Contents

Dedication	4
Acknowledgements	5
What Others Are Saying...	7
My Story	11
Preface: The journey to becoming a woman of strength	15
Part 1: Relationships	
Chapter 1: Ruth and Naomi – The Daughter Role	21
Chapter 2: Ruth and Naomi – The Mother Role	37
Chapter 3: Mary and Elizabeth	55
Part 2: Character	
Chapter 4: The Proverbs 31 Woman	73
Chapter 5: Five Cowards and a Strong Woman	93
Part 3: Leadership	
Chapter 6: Deborah – Intimacy	115
– Devotion	121
– Response	131
– Heart for the Next Generation	140
– Strength	148
Epilogue	153
Appendix	155

Dedication

Dedicated to Miriam Thea

Acknowledgements

Writing a book is something I never thought I would do. However, here it is, from my heart, to hopefully help women grow in their strength in God.

My thanks go firstly to my mum who set me, as a young girl, on the track of becoming a woman of strength. She is amazing.

To my husband for believing I could do this and to my children for their willingness to share this journey of leadership with us.

Of course, this book would be impossible without Team BCC. I'm grateful for their support in so many ways and for allowing me to be me.

To our good friends at River who have also believed in me and helped make this book a reality.

Thank you!

What Others Are Saying...

"There is a drought in the British Church: a lack of women in leadership. This book is like water in a parched desert. Refreshing and inspiring, Becky Galloway challenges women to rise up and embrace their God-given calling.

James and Becky Galloway lead the incredible Breathe City Church in the heart of England. It exemplifies the attractional missional model, reaching people across all generations and winning souls at a rapid rate. Every week they have the privilege of seeing Christ transform lives. Together they have built an environment where people are accepted, believed in and helped to fulfil their potential. You will hear some of their incredible stories within these pages.

Becky is refreshingly honest. Her writing style is easy to read and she quickly draws you into her world. She dispels many of the myths surrounding women in leadership, then with wisdom and courage builds a biblical and personal perspective that will challenge you to think higher.

Becky is quietly confident and secure. We think the best way to describe her is 'convinced'. She is convinced of who she belongs to, convinced of what she's called to do and convinced of what's important in life. You will sense her love for God, her family and the local church she leads.

Every woman who aspires to be in leadership or is serious about making a difference in this world should read this book."
Gary and Nikki Rucci, Area Leaders London and East, Assemblies of God Great Britain

"*'She is clothed with strength and dignity'* (Proverbs 31:25). Becky's heart of strength clearly comes through her writing. It is a heart of deep love and compassion for God's people and for those not yet in the Kingdom. God gives the command clearly in Scripture to be strong and courageous. Becky has responded in obedience and set out on a courageous journey to build and restore. Her passion for linking generations of women relationally has been key in unlocking a network of women where strength can flow from woman to woman. It is enabling women to reach their potential and grow in strength and love for God – in turn helping them to dramatically influence their world for good.

James and Becky are a tremendous couple who walk the talk with integrity and passion. Side by side in ministry, they have given themselves to encouraging the wider body of Christ. We have been privileged to be recipients of their friendship and encouragement in our own journey of building the local church. Our hope is that you will be encouraged not only by what Becky has written, but by the stories of hope and transformation contained in this book."

Martin & Rachel Ball, St George's, Newcastle-under-Lyme

"As a woman in ministry I love seeing women step out and take new ground for the Kingdom. *Called: the journey to becoming a woman of strength* is a great tool for helping women firstly see that they have a lot to offer in church ministry and then also to enable them to have the confidence to step out in areas that might have been unheard of not so long ago. Becky unpacks lessons learned from some much-loved characters in the Bible and shows us God's heart towards His daughters. The feminine

heart of God needs to be expressed and this book points us towards the potential God has placed within each one of us."
Dee Cook, Senior Pastor, NCLC

"Since starting the Cross Rhythms ministry in the early eighties, Kerry and I have always been open to what we call 'Kingdom collaboration'. This is easier understood than practiced, because those taking part have to be secure enough to be able to see the purposes of God as bigger than just their own ministry and then be generous enough to 'sow' into another's life or ministry. Becky is that kind of Christian. As a church leader, my most important function is to encourage our community to find their godly purpose. Productive and generous leadership is like fathering and mothering in both the natural and spiritual. Both are essential for a healthy community. I've worked with Becky on a large project and found that she is a woman of her word and a person of integrity. She is more than a mother (and I cannot stress how important that role is). She is a disciple and daughter of God in her own right and a Kingdom establisher. Her vulnerability attracts broken people to her and builds confidence for the healing work of the Holy Spirit to touch deep wounds. Her support of her husband James is the most important 'collaboration' and through the wonderful battles of building the Kingdom, Becky is faithful. Be encouraged as you read."
Chris and Kerry Cole, Founders of Cross Rhythms

"All the best books flow from a life shaped by the truth they seek to communicate. This is one of those. Becky's journey is the living illustration that makes these vital biblical truths accessible and within the reach of every woman who reads this inspirational book."

Stephen Matthew, Associate Pastor, Life Church, Bradford

My Story

For many years I have personally journeyed through the process of becoming a woman of strength. Along this journey I have met other women engaged in this same pursuit. Some are finding the journey easier than others but all, I think, would agree that it involves many challenges along the way!

One evening, whilst delivering a session entitled "Mothers in Ministry", one of my fellow leaders said, "Becky, this should really be a book." I delivered the session and went on to deliver another session to our core leaders called "Mothers in Leadership". At the end of that session another trusted "BCCer" came to me with tears in her eyes and said, "Book ... all I can say is 'book'. You need to expand that Deborah stuff and write a book."

I was a little blown away to say the least! But here I am sharing with you my journey – one that I pray encourages and challenges you to become that woman of strength that I believe all us females are called to become.

I write from a place of obedience to our God in the hope that my musings and experiences may encourage another who is also on this journey of serving God, motherhood and the rest!

My two wonderful sons are now nearly 10 and 7 and recently we discovered that God had decided to bless us with another of His "best gifts" (Psalm 127:3 MSG). "Galloway Junior" is to join us later this year. Both of my children, born in a dark period of our lives, were gifts from God that got me through some tough times. I thank God that He gave me these precious gifts during such challenging times in this journey we call life. I thank God for them every day.

Naturally speaking, neither of my children should be here. Sparing you some of the details, after two long labours both of their hearts stopped and emergency C-Sections saved their lives and probably mine too. My youngest was born with a mark the shape of a thumb print over his heart – a sign, we believe, that God healed his tiny heart. On the evening after the birth of my first child, left alone in the hospital, scared, emotional and devastated at such a horrific birth, I believe I had a visit from an angel.

I asked the morning shift, "Who was the nurse on duty last night?" After I had described her, I was told, "There was no nurse like that on duty last night." This "nurse" had sat beside my bed and looked at the baby's wristband. "Caleb," she said, "strong and determined, partner of Joshua, they entered the Promised Land." What an amazing gift God chooses to "reward" us with (Psalm 127:3 NIV) when he blesses us with children

As I'm sure any mother would agree, my kids are everything to me. We have this assumption that no one feels the way about their kids as we do about ours. It's not true. Every child is precious and a gift from God. I would be happy and fulfilled all the days of my life if I only spent all my time caring for my children.

The tension that I face – and hope to unpack in this book – is that God has placed a calling on my life to be a mother and a leader also – to be a woman of strength who handles motherhood and leadership well. You may not be a mother but nevertheless face the same daily challenge of rising up to be all God has called you to be. And as we all probably know only too well, if it's God's calling then you can't get away!

Prior to having children I was working as a Town Planner part time and serving as a volunteer in my church part time too. My husband, James, was employed full time in the church. We were both full-on, serving in the house, working alongside James' parents and trying to establish a church plant in Cardiff. We did everything from fliering to cleaning, working with students to managing church finances, but our main focus was youth work.

When I became pregnant with my first child the comments and opinions began. "You won't be able to carry on doing all that you're doing now ... You're going to have to slow down ... It won't be fair to take the baby to all those meetings ... You're going to be so tired!"

How helpful! I felt like the eyes of the world were upon us as we embarked on this journey. We were leading a growing youth ministry that spanned all across South Wales, working with many churches, leaders and youth leaders. I felt there was a kind of "Let's watch and see what they are going to do now" attitude hanging over this season in my life.

I didn't share my heart or my plans with anyone for fear of rejection, until one day the person I was closest to on our team had a bit of a wobble. She was also feeling the pressure and probably thinking, "Am I going to have a double work load when Becky has this baby?" That day something came out of my mouth as we stood outside Boots the Chemist on Queen Street in Cardiff and it became my motto, something that I still live by today:

"We are called as a family".

It is this motto that inspired the title of this book.

I have tried to live by this because I so believe it. It is the basis of every ministry decision I make.

Recently, an older visiting minister to our church asked me a strange question: "Becky, you haven't asked me why my daughters aren't in my leadership team."

"Oh!" I replied politely, "I'm sorry, I didn't realise you had daughters. Why *aren't* they on your team?"

I expected him to explain that they didn't carry the gift of leadership, or maybe he was going to tell me a sad story that they had fallen away from God. His answer, however, shocked me and is another reason for writing this book. "Well Becky," he said, "they have children and, you know, mothers in leadership – it's a complicated business."

Everything within me wanted to cry out, "No! You've got it all so wrong!" Politely I nodded, but inside my resolve became more determined to dispel this myth that seems to invade some church circles.

When I read the Great Commission I don't see a sub-clause saying, "...unless you have children." As far as I understand Scripture, we are all called to serve God in whatever capacity He leads us to.

I hope this book will encourage you and give you the permission and freedom to do just that.

PREFACE

The Journey to Becoming a Woman of Strength

So what does a "woman of strength" look like? My definition may look different to other people's, but to me it is encapsulated in Proverbs 31:25:

"She is clothed with strength and dignity; she can laugh at the days to come."

This describes a woman who is in control! All too often I meet women whose lives are in chaos. They're disorganised, full of unhelpful relationships and dictated to by addictions or unhealthy mindsets.

These women, sadly, are not clothed with strength or dignity and they are more likely to cry or despair about the days ahead rather than laugh. How far from what God created us to be!

What was Woman called to be originally? She was created because Man wasn't complete without her. Many have tried to describe the word used in Genesis 2:18 – "helper" or "help meet" to help define a woman's purpose. The word "helper" is translated from the Hebrew word *azar*. It occurs around 80 times in the Old Testament and is mainly used to refer to God as a helper. So this is not a "helper" such as a school monitor who helps his or her teacher with a task. Nor is it a piece of equipment that helps someone to complete a task. Rather this is a divine "help" – the type of help that God Himself gives. Wow! If we truly grasp this, how could a woman ever feel insignificant?

For the woman who struggles with her value, an understanding of this scripture dispels any myths! Both men and women are valuable. Both were intentional in God's plan and both are integral to His purpose for Planet Earth. It saddens me that so many women struggle with this basic concept of their intrinsic value. This book doesn't focus on that as I hope and believe that "value" is a basic principle that any woman should grasp as they read Scripture. This book looks at the next step, which is moving into all God has called us to be.

I believe both men and women alike are called to be warriors of strength in the faith. I hope that this book will help people to realise that and move towards it. The book is organised into three parts –all of which I believe are important in the journey towards strength.

The first section looks at key relationships. We will focus on some biblical characters who displayed the type of relationships that can be helpful on this journey. *Ruth and Naomi* exemplify a mother-daughter relationship that is necessary for teaching and training the next generation of women. *Mary and Elizabeth* display a healthy peer-to-peer relationship that is uncommon today. There are many other women in the Bible we could learn from, such as Hannah and Peninnah, whose relationship was unhelpful but could have been so positive if Peninnah had a different attitude. My great friend Nikki Rucci preaches an amazing message on these two ladies!

Of course, the husband/wife relationship is integral to the journey of any married woman becoming all that God has called her to be. However, as not all readers will be married, I have not explored this relationship in depth, but just added a quick guide for blokes and a bullet point reminder for us women to help guide us towards healthy male/female relationships. This subject, of course, could be a book in itself!

The second section goes on to look at our character. I believe that character is really the heartbeat of strength. Character is often overlooked in favour of gifting, but without character gifting really has no substance. It will not last or stand the test of time if it is not backed by character. Developing character takes a lifetime. It's hard work, challenging, sometimes painful, but always worth the journey. This section focuses on two characters, one from the Old Testament, who may have been fictitious but is nevertheless helpful in training us, and another from the New Testament who stands out to me amongst a host of other personalities who seem to have failed the character test.

Lastly, we come to look at the call of leadership and the challenges that face us as women and also as mothers. This really is the heartbeat of this book. I passionately believe it is possible to be a great leader *and* a great mother and I hope this section helps you to step up to become all you have been called to be!

Also included within this book are personal stories from just a few of my nearest and dearest "women of strength". These are fellow BCCers whose journeys I have witnessed. They have faced challenges and overcome them. They stand strong, although aware they have not yet made it, as mighty warriors in the faith. They are examples to me and my family. I love doing life with them and pray that you will also be inspired by their stories.

PART 1:

Relationships

PART I.

CHAPTER 1

Ruth & Naomi
THE DAUGHTER ROLE

One of my favourite books of the Bible is Ruth. It provides us with an amazing model of a mother/daughter style relationship. Of course, the two main characters, Naomi (mother) and Ruth (daughter), were not naturally mother and daughter. They were mother and daughter-in-law. But I believe the book exists, amongst other reasons, to provide us with a healthy model of the older/younger woman relationship in church life.

We have used the "Ruth/Naomi" model extensively across our women's programmes at Breathe City Church. Residents in our *Stronger* programme – a residential facility for vulnerable young women – have a mentor who is their "Naomi" and they are encouraged to take on a "Ruth" role. Mentors are trained from the book of Ruth so that they understand how they can best mentor their mentees. We have another non-residential discipleship programme for young women called PR31 and, again, young women are assigned a mentor and a Ruth/Naomi type relationship is established.

You may think this seems a bit "set up" and premeditated. Surely relationships are something that should happen naturally? Well, yes, in an ideal world. However, we live in a far from ideal world and often in church life older women don't mix with younger women and vice versa. Younger women may not understand the "Ruth/Naomi" concept and thus not seek out these relationships and older women may feel that those younger women wouldn't want their involvement in their lives anyway. I know that growing up I had no specific Naomi character in my life and, especially in my older teenage years and early 20's, I would have benefitted from such a relationship.

Interestingly, what we have seen develop at BCC over the years are relationships that are not necessarily defined by age, but by spiritual maturity. Often mentors may only be a few years older or even the same age as those they are mentoring. Spiritual maturity isn't always defined by age.

The book of Ruth falls directly after the book of Judges, although chronologically it was set in the same time frame. The opening line of the book tells us that people were living in a generation when judges ruled the land. There was no king and, as so often happens when there is a lack of leadership, things had fallen into chaos. It is no surprise then, that there was a famine in the land of Judah. Naomi's family were therefore moving from Bethlehem in Judah to Moab, presumably to pursue a better life.

Bethlehem means "the house of bread". Generally, it was a very fertile region, but because of the lack of leadership and management it had fallen into famine. A side note here: let's just dwell on that – people moving from the "house of bread". Another meaning of the word "bread" is "God" – so Bethlehem is the house of God. People were moving from the "house of God" because there was no food! What a warning to those of us who are leaders: it's our responsibility to provide food, spiritual food that will nourish our people and help them grow. Otherwise, to be honest, we have no right to complain if people leave our church! (It's always good to question yourself as a leader when people decide to leave your church. Was it because they were not being fed?)

So facing a scenario of possible death through lack of food, Elimelech, Naomi's husband (whose name means "my God is King") moves his family to Moab. The name Naomi means "lovely and pleasant". Names are important in the Bible, so here we see "my God is King" and "lovely and pleasant" leaving the "house of God" to move to Moab, some 50 miles to the south east of Bethlehem.

This was possibly not the wisest decision to make since the Moabites worshiped a god called Chemosh rather than Yahweh. Elimelech's decision to move away from the "house of bread" found him in a strange land whose people worshipped strange gods and where both his sons would marry women from Moab. The consequences of this were massive: no Moabites or their sons were allowed to enter the assembly of the Lord.

Elimelech (my God is King) makes a decision that means his grandchildren to come – the next generations – would not be able to worship his God, assuming his descendants married women from Moab. Who would have thought that such a small move of 50 miles could have such long lasting and devastating effects! This again is a reminder to us, that we ensure decisions we take are in line with the Word of God. I want to do everything within my power to ensure that my boys marry girls from the house of bread!

As we read on through the first chapter of Ruth we find that

Elimelech dies, his sons marry Moabite women and within 10 years they are dead too! It makes me think: I wonder if moving away from the house of bread can cause death? I think it's so important that we position both ourselves and our children in the house of bread rather than in a land of Moab! I address this in more detail in later sections of this book.

Towards the end of Ruth 1 we see Naomi make the decision to return to Bethlehem. How wise to return to the house of bread. God always has the door open for us.

One of Naomi's daughter-in-laws, Orpah, decides to stay in Moab, but Ruth chooses to accompany Naomi back to Bethlehem. It is this journey that we will now focus on in this section to help us understand the importance of, and how to build, those all important relationships that will aid us in the journey of becoming the strong woman of God that He has called us all to be.

RUTH AND NAOMI: THE DAUGHTER ROLE

Let's begin by looking at Ruth, the daughter in this story. A daughter is something all women are, both naturally and spiritually, so I believe we can all learn from the lessons drawn from Ruth. I am going to focus on four of these lessons.

LESSON 1: CLING

"...but Ruth clung to her." (Ruth 1:14)

When my sister moved to Stoke on Trent a few years ago, I had the privilege of taking my niece swimming every week. While my boys were in lessons we'd go into the pool together. For a while she wasn't very confident; it was a new pool and she couldn't touch the bottom. Clinging is what my niece used to do to me in that pool! Anyone who has had children who are scared of water will identify with this. It's a "cling on for dear life"; a "don't leave me, you are my safety and security" thing. There was no way my niece was going to be "un-clung" from me!

It appears to be the same here with Ruth and Naomi. Her sister, her own flesh and blood, was turning back to return home, but there was no way that Ruth was. We see her emotional plea, so similar to my niece's: "Aunty Becky, don't let me go, I'll drown."

Ruth 1:16-18:

"But Ruth replied, 'Don't urge me to leave you or to turn back from you. Where you go I will go, and where you stay I will stay. Your people will be my people and your God my God. Where you die I will die, and there I will be buried. May the Lord deal with me, be it ever so severely, if anything but death separates you and me.' When Naomi realised that Ruth was determined to go with her, she stopped urging her."

I wonder why she was so adamant to go with Naomi? She had known her 10 years or thereabouts, which is a fair while to build a good relationship, but she had known her sister and Moab all her life. Presumably she had other family relations living in Moab too, maybe even her own parents? Yet she wanted to sacrifice all this and go to a strange land with a woman of no blood relation.

There must have been a reason why!

Perhaps she had witnessed her mother-in-law's faith in her God? Perhaps she had seen something she didn't want to let go of?

Remember, Naomi was "pleasant and lovely". Ruth would also have met Elimelech and got to know "my God is King".

Perhaps she had heard stories of Bethlehem, the house of bread, and wanted to experience this life for herself? Perhaps she had caught a glimpse of the true and living God and just wasn't letting go?

As daughters then, what can we learn from this? Maybe we should have the same attitude as Ruth and cling to the things of God? Maybe, like Ruth, we should be willing to sacrifice tradition, upbringing and family, if needed, in order to follow God? Maybe we should listen to the voice of God rather than the voice of our peers and be committed to following His calling for our lives?

When we were in the process of moving from Cardiff to Stoke on Trent I was reading one of my favourite books, *Fight like a Girl* by Lisa Bevere. This quote summed up what was happening and how I was feeling:

"People are pleading with you from the beach, 'Don't go any farther I need you! Don't leave me behind. Just stay a little longer.' Your heart is drawn by the water, but you feel compelled to stay with those on the shore. It sounds harsh, but you must turn from their pleas and embrace the water. It is the only way you will ever truly be able to help them."

Interestingly, several years later, I read this to one of our girls during her detox from heroin. She was feeling the same way.

I wonder how many other people feel it too – trapped in the land of Moab – a land that doesn't serve God? At this point, the house of bread seems but a dream, but then along comes a Naomi with the promise of strength to help us. If a Naomi comes your way, then I urge you to cling to her! If you need a Naomi in the situation you're in right now, get yourself along to a good church and find one or maybe several. You'll recognise them because they will be the ladies with the look of experience on their faces that show they have faced some storms in life. Yet they will be "pleasant and lovely". If they are a true Naomi, they will be happy for you to journey with them.

LESSON 2: CHOOSE

Don't you think the mother-in-law/daughter-in-law relationship is a strange one? So many people struggle with it. To me, the uniqueness of this relationship is found at its height during and after child birth. My mother-in-law was a great support to me during the birth and the early years of my first two children. She lived locally and often called in to help me. She was amazing at cleaning my house during those early weeks. However, when it came to looking after my baby I found some of her tips interesting! Not wrong, just *different*.

I have a closer relationship with my own mother. I am her daughter. A trust exists that occurs naturally between a mother and a child. Here was the woman who cared for me when I was a baby. Her words of advice and wisdom carried far more weight than my mother-in-law's, just because of who she was. Now I am sure much of my mother-in-law's advice was good, but she wasn't my mother.

If I was in a situation where I didn't have my own mother around, I wonder if I would have chosen to adopt a different viewpoint on my mother-in-law's advice? I hear of women who have closer relationships with their mother-in-law than they do their own mother. So perhaps, although not easy, it is possible to *choose* to be a daughter.

This is what Ruth did. She chose to become Naomi's daughter. She had no obligation to Naomi, but chose to follow her to Bethlehem.

The English dictionary seems to have three possible definitions of a daughter:

1. A female offspring.
2. A female descendant.
3. A female closely connected with a certain environment, or, another version says, a person related as if by the ties binding a daughter to a parent.

This third definition says to me that it is possible to choose to be a daughter. At BCC we often talk about "sons and daughters of the House", meaning men and women, girls or boys who have been spiritually born into our church. Some churches plant "daughter" churches. A country may have a "daughter" town.

A natural daughter has no choice about being a daughter – she just is. She can choose to build that relationship or not. But even if she moves millions of miles away and disowns her parents, she is still a daughter. But a daughter who *chooses* to be a daughter must take on, and work at, the characteristics of a natural daughter. This list is not exhaustive, but she needs to:

- Choose to trust
- Choose to learn
- Choose to mimic the behaviour of the parent
- Choose to honour and respect
- Choose to love
- Choose to obey
- Choose to listen
- Choose to spend time with the parent

Ruth & Naomi: The Daughter Role

A Ruth aspiring to be a Naomi

Ruth so clearly put these principles into action. By the second and third chapters we see Naomi and Ruth in a mother–daughter scenario, where all of the above attributes come into play and Ruth responds to her and accepts Naomi's advice (Ruth 2:22-23). In accepting her advice she ends up living her dream and making history – but more on that later!

LESSON 3: FOLLOW
I've touched on this briefly above, that in choosing to be a

daughter you are choosing to follow. Just watch any little girl. No one teaches them to dress up in Mummy's heels and jewellery and try a bit of lippy on, but they do it! It's slightly worrying when your sons do this – but the less said about that the better! We recently had our annual fashion show at Breathe City Church as part of the Woman programme. One of our ladies brought her daughter with her, only nine years old. She was probably the youngest there and I loved the fact that she wanted to be there. She is following the mothers in the house! She was asked if she'd like to join our volunteer team of models. Being quite tall for her age she could get away with wearing ladies' size 8 clothes.

She stole the show!

Not in the inappropriate, "over glamorised" way in which some child models are presented. She didn't wear make-up or high heels; she wore no jewellery; she was simply beautiful as herself – a Ruth aspiring to be a Naomi. She knew where to walk, how to walk, where to pose for a photo and how the attract the crowd to buy the clothes.

Did anyone teach her? No, she just followed.

Isn't it interesting that this book of the Bible is named after the follower, not the one who went first? It is often the follower that people admire. Think of Jonathan and his armour bearer. My husband has recently published his book, *The Spirit of the Purple Cow,* on this subject of "followship" – an unknown word in the English language – how interesting's that?!

So we see Ruth refusing to go back to the land of Moab, even though it was her home, and wanting to follow Naomi. *Followship* often takes you to strange and unknown lands, areas where you may not dare to venture alone.

Ruth was from Moab. The Moabites followed foreign gods and had never heard of the God of Naomi. But Ruth was willing to recklessly abandon the gods of her youth and pledge to follow Naomi's God. If you are choosing to follow, there may need to be some reckless abandonment that goes on! You may need to leave behind your habits, your lifestyle, your friends, your comfort zone.

I believe God calls us to a life of reckless living. Not in an unwise, un-thought-through way, but in an "abandoning it all for God" way. I love John 12:25 from the Message version of the Bible:

"In the same way, anyone who holds on to life just as it is destroys that life. But if you let it go, reckless in your love, you'll have it forever, real and eternal."

With reckless abandon Ruth chose to put aside her ambitions. I am sure, like any young woman, she would have desired to marry again and have children. But her mother-in-law clearly lays it out for her: there is no hope of another husband from me!

Ruth1:12-13:

"Return home, my daughters; I am too old to have another husband. Even if I thought there was still hope for me – even if I had a husband tonight and then gave birth to sons – would you wait until they grew up? Would you remain unmarried for them? No, my daughters. It is more bitter for me than for you, because the Lord's hand has gone out against me!"

At the end of Ruth 1 we already see the effects of Ruth's commitment to follow.

Verse 22 says that they were, *"...Arriving in Bethlehem as the barley harvest was beginning."*

Barley was always the first grain to ripen. In other words,

they had arrived at the beginning of God's provision. Each feast day of Israel was associated with a harvest and Passover was associated with the barley harvest. Passover is a symbol of God's protection of His chosen people. Apparently, barley also represents "overcomers" and Naomi and Ruth certainly were. So this verse says so much: provision, protection and overcoming. This is where Ruth and Naomi landed themselves! Just as we might be unaware, as we make steps into foreign lands (maybe a new job, new territory, a new challenge, a new place in God), God has already prepared for our arrival to coincide with barley harvest time. What an encouragement!

At BCC we have been privileged to experience weekly decisions of people turning to Jesus. One such decision was made by a young girl who I have already mentioned in this book. She is one of my heroes. She gets saved and her life gets transformed. She begins to experience harvest in her life: happiness, fulfilment, right living, good friends, obstacles overcome and breakthroughs achieved. Her mother was slightly sceptical at first about her daughter's new found faith, but slowly began to notice the harvest in her daughter's life. Before long she cannot deny it and even begins to notice a harvest over spilling into their family.

Guess what?

She decides to follow her daughter to the house of bread and shortly afterwards begins to experience harvest in her own life. Don't you just love it?! Isn't this why we do what we do as Christians?

By the second chapter we see Ruth becoming a "mini Naomi". She sees Naomi pull herself up from her grief and pain and decides to follow suit instead of moping at home about the loss of a husband and the trials of a new city. One morning she gets up and states to her mother in law:

"I'm going to work; I'm going out to glean among the sheaves, following after some harvester who will treat me kindly." (Ruth 2:2 MSG)

Here we see the fulfilment of followship. No longer does Ruth need to cling to Naomi, just as my niece one day decided to swim across that pool by herself. Ruth decides to put into practice what she's seen.

LESSON 4: WORK HARD

Throughout the book of Ruth we observe a Ruth who is happy to work hard. My mum is always telling me not to work so hard! I think it's natural for a mother to be concerned that her daughter is overdoing it, but mother, wouldn't you prefer a daughter who works hard rather than one who is lazy? The Bible issues many warnings about being lazy and personally, as a mother and a daughter myself, at this stage in my life lazy is not something that's an option! Hard work is commended in the Bible and Ruth is certainly a good role model for us to follow on this subject.

As we are talking about relationships here, let's just think about what would happen in a relationship where one person is lazy and the other works hard. It's not fair! Before long the hard worker will have had enough of their lazy partner. Listen, if you are aspiring to be a Ruth, don't imagine that once you find your Naomi it's going to be an easy ride. Relationships are two-way. We shall explore this further when we come on to look at Naomi.

Even from the start of this journey Ruth commits to hard

work. You and I would think nothing of travelling 50 miles but, for Ruth and Naomi, this journey was to be on foot and carrying everything they owned. That journey would have been very lonely for Naomi, filled with hopelessness, aware of her loss of social standing, and the fear of returning to find her home town a worse place than the place she'd left. It reminds me of the story of the prodigal son.

Ruth took on the job of accompanying her on this journey. Maybe she even had to encourage Naomi, who was now calling herself "bitter and empty" rather than "pleasant and lovely". How would you fancy a journey with "bitter and empty"? Doesn't sound like fun to me – more like hard work!

But shortly after their arrival in Bethlehem Ruth is ready to go out and work. This cannot have been easy, but God rewarded her immediately. She may not have understood the reward at the time, but later in the story we find out what it is.

In Ruth 2:3 we read the phrase, *"As it turned out..."* Don't you love it when God puts in a little "as it turned out" or, in some translations, "it just so happened"? It's like God has got it planned all along, if we'll just step out in willingness. How could God have intervened if she'd sat at home all day doing nothing? She takes a step, God takes a step and, in the great board game called life, it's a step closer to her destiny. Her fellow workers testified of her, *"She has worked steadily from morning till now"* (Ruth 2:7).

By Ruth 3:11 we see her receive the great compliment, *"Everyone in this town knows what a courageous woman you are."* Wow! What a compliment. I would love that to be said of me! I wonder if it was this courageousness that caused God to choose Ruth to begin the family tree of Jesus Himself?

Being courageous is overcoming obstacles, hurts, insecurities, the things that hold us back, standing out from the crowd, stepping up and generally making that scary decision to move out with no reassurance that it will definitely work out!

We will never be courageous if we are not willing to get our heads down and work hard.

As daughters we need to understand that now is our time for hard work – there is work to be done, a home, street, community, city, nation to be won for Jesus! No time for rest – there's a harvest to glean!

Later in this book we will look at Proverbs 31 entitled "the wife of noble character". This is this exact same wording that Ruth's husband, Boaz, uses at the end of the story to describe her (Ruth 3:11).

Will you be described as someone of noble character for your hard work?

I'd like to be.

CHAPTER 2

Ruth & Naomi

THE MOTHER ROLE

We now turn to look at the mother role in this relationship between Ruth and Naomi. Remember, the "mother" may not necessarily be older in years, although it's normally more helpful if she is, but she will certainly be "older" in her faith in God – not necessarily represented by the number of years she's been a Christian, but by the level of maturity she has reached.

BCC is a relatively young church; we don't have a wealth of older and more experienced Christians. And since you can't cheat time, many of our mentors are only just in front of the girl they are mentoring. I have included at the end of this book an appendix containing information we use for our mentees and mentors on the Stronger programme. Although it is very specific to that particular programme, I hope you may find it a useful resource.

So let's turn to look at the characteristics of a mother mentor and once again pull out some lessons.

LESSON 1: INITIATIVE
Ruth 1:6-7: *"One day she got herself together ... And so she started out from the place she had been living."*

One day! "One days" are important days, days where life-changing decisions are made; days when you actually do something about your situation. Naomi made a start! She used her initiative. It would have been easier, more comfortable and certainly would have saved face if she had stayed in Moab. Moab was the place where she had been physically living. But where had she been living emotionally and spiritually?

I think "the place where she had been living" was a place of death and grief, a foreign land where God was not honoured. She could have continued to dwell there, but she chose to pull herself together.

I commend girls applying to the Stronger programme for taking those first steps in "getting themselves together".

If you are aspiring to be a mother or if you are a mother naturally, sometimes you may need to give yourself a little talking to and say, "Oi woman, pull yourself together!"

Don't you just love hearing stories of women who have conquered so much – the battles they have come through and the difficulties they have overcome? If you are feeling that you can't overcome, be encouraged! You can!

"You groped your way through that murk once, but no longer. You're out in the open now. The bright light of Christ makes your way plain." (Ephesians 5:8 MSG)

We see a dissatisfaction begin to rise in Naomi in Ruth 1:6: *"When she heard ... that the Lord had come to the aid of his people by providing food for them..."* she began to wonder, "What would it be like in Bethlehem?" Whenever you feel dissatisfaction rise up it means it's time to do something. It may be due to an unjust cause, a particular situation or just the recognition that there is no "bread" here any more. Whatever it is, in that situation *do something*; because if you don't, either you will die or others will die.

I love causes like the A21 campaign, the organisation Compassion, Christians Against Poverty and other programmes that have been birthed out of a dissatisfaction with the status quo.

Any cause that involves life and death is worth fighting for.

A while ago we had an awesome leader with us who prophesied over us that we were confronting the spirit of death, particularly through the ministry of Stronger. It dawned on me that this ministry, and all we are doing at BCC, is actually rescuing people from the claws of death. Proverbs 14:27 says, *"The fear of the Lord is a fountain of life, turning a man from the snares of death."*

As I then sat in one of BCC's City Gatherings, I watched ten amazing individuals stand and testify why they were about to go through the waters of baptism. There were two amazing stories that stood out of people being rescued from the claws of death; tear-jerking stories told of lives totally transformed as, individually, these people had found God.

That same week we were also privileged to have with us Canon J. John who, after preaching, invited people to make a first time decision to follow Jesus. Many people made their way to the front of the auditorium to make the life-changing decision that would bring them from the claws of death into life in all its fullness.

Life and Death is a serious business and initiative stands between them. Naomi was bold enough to make a start, take the initiative and move from the situation of death she found herself in. How often do we miss an opportunity because we haven't got the courage to pull ourselves together and take that initiative?

LESSON 2: UNSELFISH LOVE

I do struggle with the term "mentor". It doesn't seem to quite encapsulate what we find here in Naomi. A mentor speaks of someone whose job it is to look after someone, maybe in the workplace, such as a more experienced factory worker training a new factory worker. Or of someone in the education system who is paid to come alongside a student to support them.

Naomi is so much more than that. She is a *mother*. A mother wants her daughter to go higher and further than she was ever able to go and when her daughter achieves it she won't feel a hint of jealousy, only pride and satisfaction.

I understand that we have all had different experiences of natural mothers. Yours may have been good, bad or indifferent. I have tried to study the first mother in the Bible, Eve.

It must have been a man who wrote Genesis because what I find is that Eve gives birth to two sons, then in the next verse they are adults with their own careers! This is not very helpful when you are trying to study motherhood! The only information we are given is, *"I have brought forth a man"* or as the Message phrases it in Genesis 4:1, *"I have gotten a man."*

When I think back to the birth of my two boys, it would have been rather strange if the first thing I said was, "I've gotten a man!" More likely I said, "It's a baby boy!" When my husband went to break the news to the rest of the family, I would imagine he said, "It's a boy!" He may have said, "I've gotten a boy – YES!" But it's very unlikely he would have said, "I've gotten a man." Babies aren't born as men and women, they are born as babies. The process that takes place over the next 18 years is what causes them to become a man or a woman.

I wonder if those two small words "brought forth" talk of Eve's journey with Cain and Abel; of loving and supporting them to become men? I would hope to be able to say on each of my sons' 18th birthdays, "With God's help, we have brought forth a man.'" To me, that would make sense. I may be totally off beam but, nevertheless, Cain and Abel obviously grew up to be men and, by implication, must have been nurtured, cared for, provided for and loved.

Let's turn back to Naomi's love and remember that these girls were not her natural children. She had chosen to be a mother to both Ruth and Orpah. In Ruth 1:8 she tells her daughters-in-law to go back to their homes. She prays a blessing on them as they go. She prays they will find new husbands. She explains it will be better for them to go home. She understands that it will not be an easy journey for them, but her love for them compels her to encourage them not to join her. If she had been selfish, I am sure she would have requested these girls to come with her. The journey would have been more fun with three. It would be lonely living in Bethlehem alone. And who knows, in the future they may bring her grandchildren who she would love to know.

Does this unselfish love come naturally to Naomi figures or is it something they need to work on? I believe it's all to do with the heart. Do we have God's heart for people? As a Naomi figure, I love the girls in BCC. I believe the reason I love them is because I focus on what God says about them: they are loved, cherished, precious, beautiful, overcomers, achievers, leaders and princesses. Can they be unlovable? Most definitely, sometimes! But I still love them, just as I do my own children when they misbehave.

I would argue that this type of love needs to be developed and with me it is probably something that developed over the years I worked with young people whilst living in Cardiff. I remember talking to friends about some of the young people we were working with and they used to make comments such as, "They just need to get their lives sorted out." This may be a fair comment when you take a quick glance at some women's lives. However, we need to ask for God's heart and show a Naomi love for them.

LESSON 3: UNSHAKEABLE FAITH

When we are training mentors at BCC, we tell them that this is a two-way relationship. It's important that they share their life with the girl they are mentoring as well as vice versa. It's important that any "Ruth", or mentee, sees that "Naomi", her mentor, is not perfect. They will learn from our struggles. They may even surprise us and provide some answers to our struggles. Often their childlike faith can be so much more simple and uncomplicated than ours!

I love my kids' simple answers to the most complex of problems. I'm sure my eldest boy could sort out any church difficulties so much more effectively than James and I! He once told me it was silly that church leaders got upset when people moved from one church to another. He said, "Surely church leaders should be getting people into church who don't go to *any* church. Isn't that the whole point, Mum?" Child-like understanding. Receive it from your Ruth.

Naomi was most definitely transparent in front of Ruth:

"Don't call me Naomi," she said. *"Call me Mara, because the Almighty has made my life very bitter. I went away full, but the Lord has brought me back empty. Why call me Naomi? The Lord has afflicted me; the Almighty has brought misfortune upon me."* (Ruth 1:20-21)

The advice given to most mentors would be, "Don't show your weaknesses to those you are mentoring ... Don't be negative, only positive." But here Naomi puts her feelings on display and Ruth seems undeterred by it. We don't find her following suit and changing her name to "bitter" or "depressed". I wonder if Ruth noticed the word that Naomi used for God during her little rant? She used the name *El Shaddai* – Almighty. And here is my point: though her situation was far from perfect, though she faced some storms and couldn't imagine life being okay again, she still refered to God as her Almighty. This is what a Ruth needs to see in a Naomi – an unshakable faith and an understanding of 2 Corinthians 5:7 that, *"We live by faith, not by sight."* Everyone needs someone to whom they can go who will assure them that everything is going to be alright. The girl who's been raped needs to know it's okay; the girl who's escaped abuse needs to know she's safe; the girl who's been told she's unlovely needs to hear that she's lovely; the girl who's just lost a relative needs to know God's in control. Where are the Naomi figures to rise up and provide a rock of unshakeable faith?

I recently put a big "ask" on some Naomi women in our

church. I needed some women of unshakeable faith to stand firm. It wasn't an easy task for them because they might have to hear things that they'd prefer not to hear about. But they chose to stand firm and because of that I have witnessed many Ruths flourish.

I am not sure why, but I have never found many Naomi women in my life.

When my husband has a leadership challenge to overcome, he has a whole host of male warriors in the faith he can turn to for advice. I have only one or two women at leadership level who I consider Naomi figures.

Naomi: where are you? Please rise up!

We need your unshakeable faith!

LESSON 4: SHARED RESOURCES

Now that they are back in the "house of bread", Naomi and Ruth's situation changes to one of faith, life and hope. We don't know if Naomi had remembered that Boaz was a family relative, but using this relationship and the piece of land she had been left by her husband, she engineers a marriage between Ruth and Boaz. In Chapter 2 we see Ruth meet Boaz. Naomi recalls he's a relative known as a *kinsman redeemer*. In Bible times the kinsman redeemer was responsible for protecting the interests of needy ones in his extended family, including the redeeming of family land and the marrying of any widows. Naomi is willing to share this resource with Ruth. If Ruth had remained in Moab she would not have been entitled to this help. What we see emerge next is a typical mother-in-law matchmaking plot. It makes quite shocking reading really, but Naomi is determined to get Ruth fixed up with a good man!

You may not have a supply of kinsman redeemers to fix up any Ruths who need it, but you can certainly share your experience and wisdom in this area with them. And Ruth, listen up for a minute: *take their advice!* Male/female relationships are the biggest downfall for Ruths. I could weep for the number of beautiful young Ruths who have thrown away their destiny in God for the sake of a man who doesn't love Jesus.

I realised I may have become a bit too vocal on this subject when my youngest came home from school one day saying that a girl in his class wanted to marry him. I asked him what he said and he replied, "I told her I couldn't marry her because she didn't love Jesus." If only we could keep it that simple when we get older!

Naomi is willing to get involved to try and get Ruth back on her feet: *"One day Naomi her mother-in-law said to her, 'My daughter, should I not try to find a home for you, where you will be well provided for?'"* (Ruth 3:1). Ruths sometimes need a Naomi to take them clothes shopping, to show them how to boil an egg, to make a visit to a solicitor with them, to do some research on the Internet. Mothers are practical. I sit and help my sons with their homework. I take them to swimming lessons. I do all I can to help them be the best they can be. Naomi figures should do the same.

When we stage our large events we have a wonderful system where a stylist helps anyone who is going to be on stage to look their best. This may include advising them on outfits, colourings, or doing their hair. A while ago I noticed one of our Ruths had a flair for styling hair. Unlikely to push herself forward

I decided I would use my resources to try and help her. I am not a hairdresser so I couldn't train her, but I do have the resource of being a leader, so I asked our regular stylist if this Ruth could work alongside her. She agreed, as did the Ruth.

Sometime later we were having a *Colour Me Beautiful* session. I prompted the stylist to invite this young Ruth along. She did, but unfortunately the Ruth couldn't afford the event. The stylist (a fellow Naomi) and I put our heads together and decided to pay for her to come. We used the resources we had to help Ruth. I was delighted when I turned up at church just last week and found this young Ruth occupying the stylist's room alone (that sounds rather posh – it's just a corner!). I was due to lead the meeting. She nervously did my hair and did the most sensational job. What a delight to be involved as a Naomi in this journey!

What resources can you share with a Ruth? Time, finance, prayer, advice, a smile or simply by being someone who believes in them. We can all give something! And by the way, all of us are a Naomi to someone, so if you think this doesn't apply to you, think again!

THE PROMISE FULFILLED

What a wonderful ending this story has! Naomi's willingness to be a mother and Ruth's decision to be a daughter, combined with the grace of God, brings about Obed, meaning "servant of God". I would imagine he was a much-wanted son for Ruth and a long-awaited heir for Naomi.

Ruth is described by Naomi's friends as being *"better than seven sons"* (Ruth 3:15). That was a true accolade in those days where sons were considered to be more valuable than daughters.

I am sure you know the ending: Obed became the father of Jesse who became the father of David, the genealogy through which Jesus Himself was born on this earth.

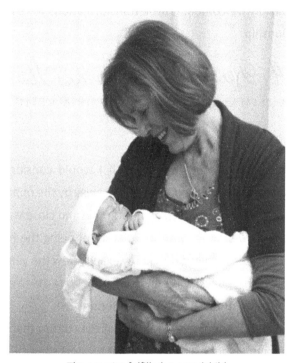

The promise fulfilled: a grandchild

I wonder if Naomi could have ever imagined such a thing when she called herself bitter! God had called Naomi to so much more than the life she was living and the same applies to you and me!

I love Psalm 9:9. This is a slight paraphrase of mine, but this is how I take it: *"You are never sorry you knocked on God's door."*

At BCC, each month we record and play a "City Transformation" video at our gatherings. These short DVDs tell the story of a life turned around by Jesus – just like that of Ruth and Naomi.

In this section, all about relationships, it's interesting to note that at some point during each of the City Transformations videos you will hear something along the lines of, "...and my friend brought me to church" or "So-and-so prayed for me" or "I was warmly welcomed." These transformations were initiated by relationship.

A Ruth & Naomi Story
JO & EMMA: STRONGER MENTOR & RESIDENT

JO'S STORY

When Pastor Becky first asked me if I would consider being Emma's mentor I was completely blown away by the opportunity to walk alongside her in such an intentional and close way. I was nervous and I definitely felt the pressure of being the first ever Stronger mentor. I really didn't know exactly how the year would turn out which, I guess, was where we both were at – we started our journey together on a common ground.

I had a very limited understanding of the culture that Em had come from and wondered exactly what support she would need. Neither of us knew the exact destination, but I was trusting God that He knew and had equipped both of us with everything required for our journey together. It's been an absolute privilege to invest time and energy and walk alongside Em as she's bravely chosen to keep walking and keep saying yes to God.

One of the biggest challenges for me has been the knowledge that, at any given time, Em could turn back and change the direction of her journey and that I have no hold over her progress or her decisions, but I hang on to knowing the power of championing her on to overcome the situations and circumstances she faces and to empower her to become all that God has created her to be. She is a true example of a girl who chose to plant herself in the House of God and flourish into a woman of God that others now look to as their example.

I think it's been important for me to know and understand that Em was never my responsibility. Ultimately she is responsible for herself before God, but I had a responsibility *to* her – to guide her, to speak truth, to be reliable, to demonstrate character and integrity when what she had known before was so different.

The journey itself has been an adventure of discovery together. Despite the mentor relationship being about Em, I have certainly grown and benefited from our intentional time together as a person. I do confess to having some control freak tendencies and sometimes I wanted to say to Em, "Don't even think about doing this, that and the other!" Sometimes this has its place, but I knew for the most part it was about facilitating her journey through those thoughts and feelings and helping her to create her own decision making processes so that she would be independent of me.

Ultimately she had to become stronger in God, not stronger in Jo.

In many of our mentor sessions it felt like getting blood out of a stone when trying to get Em to talk to me about anything meaningful. I remember one occasion, about six months in, when Em was finding life at Stronger particularly difficult. She was ready to give up. But she didn't actually verbalise any of this, which made the evening's conversation quite interesting. I think I said at one point, "I'm not leaving here until you start talking to me and telling me what's going on in your head. I don't care if it takes minutes, hours or even all night, I'm not leaving!" I did think that it could be a very long evening depending upon her response and I was genuinely prepared to stay as long as it took. I wasn't prepared to say something that I wouldn't follow through on and I think Em realised this. She did begin to talk and we began to unpack what was going on for her at that time. I found that it was important to always tell Em something about my life that was important to me, but wasn't emotionally charged. It was about demonstrating vulnerability in sharing and doing life together, but at the same time ensuring appropriateness in what I did share with her.

There has definitely been frustration and complete "Aaaarrrggghhh! What are you doing?" moments, but actually they pale into insignificance when I remember her mum getting saved and then her best friend, seeing her relationship with her son Jacob flourish and to see her taking ownership of the life that God has given her. It's like I've taken on the role of a spiritual midwife in caring for and empowering Em. I've looked on and stood alongside her as God has been forming her identity, dreams and creating space for a phenomenal future inside her – one which I've had the privilege of supporting and helping her to bring to birth over the year.

EMMA'S STORY

When Pastor Becky told me Jo was going to mentor me through my Stronger journey I was happy, as she was someone I already knew from church – although this didn't mean that I trusted her or felt that I could open up to her in any way. I think at times I made things very difficult for Jo. At first I found mentor meetings really hard. The words I wanted to say wouldn't come out and I sat in silence for a lot of the time (very awkward). But the support Jo gave me and the fact that she never gave up trying to talk to me slowly started to show me that she cared enough to keep trying and wasn't about to tell me that I wouldn't make it, like so many people before her had. My time in Stronger was by no means easy. Before even moving in I had the massive decision of leaving my two bedroom council flat in the area where I grew up. It was a place that was by no means a healthy environment for me, but it was all I had ever known. The fear of leaving what had always been and what, at the time, felt safe – what I believed to be "normal life" – was overwhelming.

It would also be life changing for my son Jacob who had to move school. Kids are great since they adjust to change a lot quicker than adults, but it was still a huge step of faith for us both.

I moved into Stronger as the first official resident on New Year's Eve 2010, having completed a detox off methadone. Everything felt a little uncertain to me. I didn't know if Jacob would like his new school; family and friends were calling me back to what had been; I was unsure how I would get a house after Stronger; I didn't know if I would even like Stronger at all!

Jo was with me through all of this. She always had a positive word for me. She challenged my negative thinking about myself and taught me to replace that with all that God says about me. We talked about goals and dreams, things that didn't seem impossible to me but reachable. I started to see that Jo was loyal to her word and would always try her best to help me.

This still did not make our mentor meetings any easier. I now see that being on drugs from the age of 15 until 21 had left me quite emotionless. All feelings had been suppressed by the drugs, so to then come off everything, start going to church (which was unknown in our family) and then do a detox was a huge thing for me. To then move to Stronger and try and talk about what was going on in my head, now that my emotions were not being suppressed by drugs, freaked my little world right out! All the things that drugs had been blocking were coming to the surface and this time I had to deal with it.

I would be so apprehensive about meeting Jo. I would sit there not looking at her at all, barely saying more than two words and then, the worst thing ever, guaranteed at the end of every single meeting, was that Jo would say, "Now we are going to pray and Em, I want you to join in!" Every time! I used to find it so difficult to pray out loud, especially if it had been a tough mentor meeting, but Jo kept going with it and would never give up on me praying. So, even if it was just, "Thank you, God," I did it every time.

Now I have the privilege of praying for other women who are having a difficult time. Had it not been for God and learning what He says about me that broke the fear that gripped me – and also Jo's consistency, even when I was so set against it – I don't think I would be in a place where I could confidently pray for others.
During my time at Stronger my relationship with God went a lot deeper. I got into my Bible more and started to ask questions and wanted to learn more. I started to rely on God and to see that my past was forgiven. By doing this, it helped me to move forward and learn to be a better mum to Jacob. I had lost a lot

of years and blamed myself daily for that but, by again changing my way of thinking and with some help, I was able to look to the future and not live in the past. Another thing to come from this was that my mum came to BCC and gave her life to Jesus! She couldn't deny the change in me and although having at first thought, "They're all bonkers!" she has now come to know and love God herself. God restored not only mine and Jacob's relationship but also mine and my mum's. Her quote the day she was baptised was, "God has given me my daughter back!"

There have been a lot of challenges along the way, from learning grace when living in a house full of girls, learning to cook properly, having to tell people my story, to things like coming back to Stronger the evening I ran back to my mum's, arms folded by the gate refusing to leave. Slowly, step by step, with help and guidance from Jo I started to change. I grew in confidence, began dealing with situations instead of running away from them and I learnt to trust in God and experience His perfect love. And, I finally let go of the past.

I have gone from being a broken, hurt girl who couldn't look at anyone let alone enjoy talking to them, to a confident, happy (most of the time), empowered princess of God – all through saying yes to Him and never giving up, no matter how much I felt like it at times.

CHAPTER 3

Mary & Elizabeth

We are looking at the role that relationships play in helping us become strong as women, mothers and leaders.

The relationship between Mary and Elizabeth is interesting to look at because here are two women who become united as friends through a common bond. Mary, the mother of Jesus, and Elizabeth, the mother of John the Baptist. They were both pregnant at the same time. It's often the case that friendships are built on a common bond, whether that is work, children being in the same class at school, going through a life experience together or, as in this situation, being pregnant at the same time.

Many women report that they remain friends forever with other women who had babies at the same time as them. It is the shared experience, the highs and the lows, the mutual understanding in the situation, and many other reasons that draw women together.

Relationships can, of course, be positive or negative and in the previous section we focused on a mother/daughter mentoring relationship. The relationship between Mary and Elizabeth is a peer relationship – perhaps the most common type of relationship we find ourselves in. From the moment we start nursery school we are encouraged to find "nice friends". As a mother I remember looking out for other "nice boys" for my sons to befriend. You invite them round for tea or take them on outings to the park together to try and help your child develop these relationships. However, there will come a time where your children will have to choose their own friendships. As mothers we understand the importance of these peer relationships and want the best for our kids. Of course, the Bible speaks such wisdom with the proverb, *"Bad company corrupts good character"* (1 Corinthians 15:33).

Relationships can be damaging or helpful to your development as a strong woman and as an adult it is sensible to choose your friends wisely. I have watched many Christians come to understand this truth who've had to go through the process of severing unhelpful relationships. I have also, as a leader, encouraged and even helped to instigate relationships that are healthy and positive.

Why do women have such a bad reputation when it comes to peer relationships?

How often have you sat in the office, the gym or a restaurant and overheard a woman backbiting about her so called "friend"? How often do we hear the sad story of one friend betraying another? I don't believe that this is how God designed things to be!

Adam and Eve were created to be in relationship. The first human beings were also created in God's likeness. This means that we too were created to be in relationship with one another. Since we were also created in God's likeness, it also means that when we backstab, betray each other, and act with jealousy, we are actually offending God.

Let's go on to explore this relationship between Mary and Elizabeth and take some examples from it. If relationships are all about shared experiences, let's look at some experiences they shared and see how they walked through these experiences together. The full story is found in Luke 1:5-57.

EXPERIENCE 1: CHOSEN

Mary and Elizabeth were both chosen to accomplish the purposes of God. Their individual purposes were different – though outworked in the same way at different times in their lives – but the common theme was that they were both *chosen*.

Do you understand that you are chosen? That there are other women with a similar "choseness" that it would be worth your while seeking out?

Zechariah, Elizabeth's husband, was carrying out his priestly duties. He was serving God and getting on with life. But all the while he was carrying the burden that he and his wife had not been able to conceive a child. Then, all of a sudden – whack!

Chosen.

Mary, a virgin engaged to be married, was also getting on with her life when – whack!

"God has a surprise for you." (see Luke 1:29)

The first point here that will help us have healthy peer relationships is to understand that we are all chosen. God has no favourites – we are all His favourites. In case you doubt that, read this:

"But you are a chosen generation, a royal priesthood, a holy nation, His own special people, that you may proclaim the praises of Him who called you out of darkness into His marvellous light;

who once were not a people but are now the people of God, who had not obtained mercy but now have obtained mercy." (1 Peter 2:9-10 NKJV)

We see no jealousy in this friendship between Mary and Elizabeth. Considering Elizabeth was "well on in years" and Mary was a "young virgin", there could have been some jealousy or resentment on Elizabeth's part. Why had she had to wait so long to have a baby? How come it had happened for Mary so quickly?

But listen to Elizabeth's beautiful attitude in Luke 1: 42-43:

"In a loud voice she exclaimed: 'Blessed are you among women, and blessed is the child you will bear! But why am I so favoured, that the mother of my Lord should come to me?'"

Wow! How do you feel when your friend comes running to you with good news? Blessed? Favoured? Or resentful and bitter? Let's choose to celebrate good news with our friends in the understanding that we are all chosen and our time will come.

The issue of having babies is a big one for women and so is the issue of getting married, but resentment and bitterness can also arise when any good fortune comes your friend's way. We can sometimes be guilty of prejudices that actually block a relationship from ever starting.

I spent a year of my life in Brecon gaining work experience as a Town Planner before I could qualify as a Chartered Town Planner. I moved to Brecon from Cardiff. I didn't know a soul, drove myself up in my little red metro with all my worldly belongings, rented a room and began a year's adventure. It was a welcome sight to find an envelope with my name on it pushed through the door of the house I was renting. It was from a colleague-to-be and read, "Me and my mates will be at the Boar's Head at 7.30pm. You are welcome to join us if you want. Nicky."

Challenge: I knew I had to do it, I needed to make friends, but I was scared!

What would they think of me?

Would these Welsh girls like me?

How would I know who they were?

Was I prepared to walk into a pub all alone and then try and make conversation with a load of strangers?

I decided to go for it. I spent a while thinking what would be best to wear ... how much make up ... what do I do with my hair? But eventually I was ready to make the short walk to the Boar's Head. As I approached the pub I saw a group of girls sat in the pub garden. "This must be them," I thought.

They were all staring at me.

Examining me.

What were they thinking?

Oh no, was I wearing the wrong thing?

They looked like they were all "girly girls" and I was wearing jeans and a hoody.

It's ridiculous isn't it, what we put ourselves through? Those girls became some great friends and Nicky remains a lifelong friend, 20 years on. I later learnt that as I walked over that bridge, one of them turned to Nicky and said, "We'll never be friends with her, she's far too posh!"

We all have the same hang ups and insecurities! Let's focus for a moment on what God says about us. Let's believe what He says and not the lies that the world feeds us. Then, just maybe, the chips on our shoulders will be removed in order for us to build good relationships. I am so glad I walked over that bridge. I am so glad Nicky didn't listen to the comments of her friends. I am sure Mary was so glad she went to visit Elizabeth. Seek out others who understand they are chosen and journey together.

EXPERIENCE 2: MIRACLE

We have two major miracles going on here. Neither of these women should have been pregnant. Elizabeth was too old and Mary was not yet married – need I say more!

I wonder if the spirit of competiveness ever entered either of their minds:

"My miracle's better than yours ... I should never have got pregnant."

"Well there was no way I could have got pregnant!"

"Gabriel visited my husband."

"Well he visited both me and Joseph, so there!"

"I'm carrying John the Baptist."

"Well beat this, I'm carrying the Saviour of the world!"

It didn't happen! All we see is that both women considered themselves blessed. If we look at Luke 1:42-44 we see that Elizabeth uses the word "blessed" four times and in verse 48 Mary says, "I'm the most fortunate woman on earth" (The Message).

We live in a competitive world and it starts from a young age. Later in this book I will talk about toddler group competiveness. It's wrong. We are each unique!

James tells us quite clearly that these are the type of worldly practices we should keep ourselves free from:

"Religion that God our Father accepts as pure and faultless

is this: to look after orphans and widows in their distress and to keep oneself from being polluted by the world." (James 1:27)

Healthy peer relationships start with us acting out the fruit of the Spirit: love, joy, peace, patience, kindness, goodness, faithfulness, gentleness and self-control. With this fruit working in our lives, our relationships are off to a good start.

Are you doubting God's miracle in your life? Do you see it in everyone else's life but not your own? Just stop a moment ... what situations do you find yourself in that naturally you shouldn't be in? That's God's miracle at work in your life. It may be in your home, your job, your family, your freedom, or your relationships.

If your friends are struggling to celebrate your miracle with you, could I urge you as nicely as possible to find some new friends? Find some others who are also experiencing God's miracle and are willing to celebrate with you.

On our journey to Stoke on Trent we lost some very good friends. They were friends who struggled to see the miracle that God was working in our lives. As much as we tried to explain it – they failed to see it. This is hard when you have a shared history and you love people. But these types of friends will not help you on your journey to becoming strong and it's sometimes time to cut ties. I am sure that if you have to do this, God will bless you as He did us and supernaturally provide you with friends who are willing to share your "now" miracle.

When James and I came to meet the existing leadership team at what was "The Bethel" we were apprehensive. We had left a great team in Cardiff. How could they be beaten? We limited God and in our minds convinced ourselves that there was no way we could have such a great team again who were also great friends. That evening a young man and his wife came up to us and said, "I'm with you heart and soul." They gave us the keys to their house. Right there and then God replaced everything we'd had to leave behind.

I love the "baby leaping" moment in Luke 1:41:

"When Elizabeth heard Mary's greeting, the baby leaped in her womb, and Elizabeth was filled with the Holy Spirit."

Look for friends with whom you can share baby leaping moments as you celebrate each other's miracles!

EXPERIENCE 3: NEW BIRTH

Mary and Elizabeth celebrated new birth together.

When there is new birth in your life, there is a reason to celebrate. When a baby is born, what do we do? Send cards and flowers, give gifts, cry with joy maybe. We celebrate. Likewise, when you have overcome something that you have struggled with, that is new birth. When God gives you fresh revelation, that is new birth.

Luke 1:57-58: *"When Elizabeth was full-term in her pregnancy, she bore a son. Her neighbours and relatives, seeing that God had overwhelmed her with mercy, celebrated with her."*

Some reading this are "full term" in what you have been carrying. When it comes to birth, others, your friends, should see God's mercy and celebrate. New birth is a private promise come to fulfilment and then the celebration goes public!

Luke 1:46-48 (MSG):

"And Mary said, I'm bursting with God-news; I'm dancing the song of my Saviour God. God took one good look at me, and look

what happened — I'm the most fortunate woman on earth!"

Elizabeth and Mary knew what it was to celebrate new birth together. But what would have happened if one of them had become offended for some reason? Perhaps the Rabbi sent Mary a bigger baby basket than Elizabeth or perhaps Elizabeth's new birth was celebrated more fully because John was born first? I know, it sounds ridiculous doesn't it? And offence is just that.

"So, chosen by God for this new life of love, dress in the wardrobe God picked out for you: compassion, kindness, humility, quiet strength, discipline. Be even-tempered, content with second place, quick to forgive an offence. Forgive as quickly and completely as the Master forgave you. And regardless of what else you put on, wear love. It's your basic, all-purpose garment. Never be without it." (Colossians 3:12-15 MSG)

We may get offended but we don't have to receive offence! We can choose not to clothe ourselves with it. I like the sound of this wardrobe talked about in Colossians. Compassion, kindness, humility, quiet strength – the list goes on. I don't know about you, but I best go home and check my wardrobe and chuck out anything that doesn't belong there in my new life in Christ!

Offence can ruin a great relationship, so deal with it quickly before it takes root. Instead, celebrate new birth in the life of others and take some time to think about what new birth God has given you now, or what new birth you are standing in faith for.

An Idiot's Guide For Blokes & A Checklist for Women

My husband suggested that I add an "idiot's guide for men", perhaps for husbands or male leaders trying to support and help women on their journey or husbands of wives who believe they are called to leadership together. However, I think this idiots' guide can also act as a resolution for us women to ensure we maintain healthly male/female relationships. God didn't create us to be in competition with each other, but to complement each other. Sadly, sometimes in church life this balance gets unbalanced. Let's make this bullet pointed as I'm aware blokes like headlines, not detail!

- We don't want to compete with you; we want to complement you. Please allow us to fulfil that God-given call on our lives
- We value you and understand that God has created you to be the head. We submit to you and ask you love us as the Bible commands (Ephesians 5:25)
- Please don't treat us as incapacitated or invalids when we are pregnant or have small children. We are sorry for the times we have used children as an excuse. We are committed to the cause of Christ and sometimes struggle to work this out alongside our mother duties. Please be patient and help us!

- Please don't box us into children's ministry and women's ministry Of course we have a heart for these areas of church life, but we also have gifting to bring to the wider church
- Together can we please place value on kids and youth programmes. They are not babysitting services to be only staffed by women! Both our young girls and boys need male and female role models. Men, please serve alongside us in these ministries. We need you!
- We apologise for when women have degraded men from the pulpit. We will always champion you! We will place value on men's ministries and pray for you.

And finally, if you are a male reading just this part, could I suggest you read the whole of this book to help you fully understand a women's heart in relationships, character and leadership? If you only have time to read one section, please look at section three which I hope will help you understand our aim to be a "Deborah" in the House of God. Thank you!

PART 2:

Character

PART I.

Let Me Tell You A Story

As we commence this section, let me tell you a story about a woman I know. She is totally amazing – the type of person you look up to and want to be like. She is beautiful both inside and out. Her strong and steadfast nature makes her so attractive. She's married with children and her husband is so supportive of her in all that she does. She has the kind of relationship with him that you don't often see these days: mutual respect and a deep love.

She runs her own Internet business making the most beautiful jewellery and unique designs of clothing. The fabrics she uses for the clothes are one-off pieces, like nothing I've ever seen before. She tells me she scours the markets of the country looking for the finest and most unusual designs. She set up the business when she was on maternity leave with her first child. Ten years on the business has done so well that she now has a small factory and employs five people. She introduced me to the girls who work for her and they all said what a great boss they have. They know they have to work hard, but she is fair. They also said that she works so hard herself that they are willing to go the extra mile for her. She's the type of boss who doesn't mind getting her hands dirty.

She's got three children. Her middle child is a monkey and he keeps her on her toes, but she always seems to handle him so well – I wish I could be more like her in the way I handle my boys. Her home always seems to be open; other children from the street are often playing in her garden and neighbours are popping in for a cup of tea. Right now she's hosting a young lady who had nowhere else to go. She seems to treat her like one of the family.

She became my friend at our local church where we both served on the kid's team together. Her husband's on the leadership team and together they are pillars in the house. I asked her one day how she did all she did, worked so hard, looked after the kids, managed church commitments and still had a smile on her face at the end of the day. She said she learnt long ago that what her father told her as a little girl was true: "I am more precious than jewels."

My first thought about this was: "What an arrogant statement, that she would think of herself so highly!" Then I looked at the Bible and read Psalm 139, which talked about how God knew me before I was born and that He even had plans for me before I was conceived – that as I grew within my mother's womb He was watching me with a smile on His face, proud as a father should be of His child; as I grew as a child He was watching and protecting me.

I also turned to the book of Jeremiah and learnt that God had plans for me, plans that only I could fulfil, plans that were good. Perhaps God would fulfil my dreams? Perhaps God would be there for me during difficult times in my life? Maybe when situations seemed disastrous, God would pull me through? But

I still questioned, why would anyone do this for me, an average girl from an average family from a (not particularly glamorous) average town, attending an average school, getting average grades, attending an average university and getting an average degree?

I'm no one special!

Or am I?

I love the diamonds on the engagement ring that James gave me as a symbol that he would love me forever. But the Bible says that God thinks I am worth more than these diamonds. Diamonds cost a lot. Not many people can afford them. Only the rich and famous seem to be draped in them. So if God says I am worth more than that, then that is amazing!

Could it be true?

The woman I introduced you to earlier has become a friend to me; a mentor and someone to look up to and aspire to be like; someone I have tried to model my life upon; someone I turn to in tough times and challenge myself as to whether I am matching up to her standards. For those who know the Bible you may have realised that we find my friend in Proverbs 31.

This section is all about character, which is so important in the journey of becoming a woman, a mother and a leader of strength. The passage I'm referring to starts at Proverbs 31:10 and reads,

"A wife of noble character who can find?" (NIV)

The Message says, *"A good woman is hard to find"* and the NKJ calls her a *"virtuous woman"*. The Amplified version explains it more fully: *"a capable, intelligent and virtuous woman"*.

If the Bible poses the question, "Who can find?" then it must mean she is rare. That's not good!

We need a generation of women who are of noble character, who are all virtuous, capable and intelligent. I have made it my aim to train our women at BCC to be this kind of woman. I now often joke that when I read that verse that ends "who can find?" I feel like going to the doors of our church and shouting out, "They are all in here! This is where you'll find them!"

I hope that as we journey together looking at some women of noble character, you too will be encouraged to develop your character to a place of strength.

CHAPTER 4

The Proverbs 31 Woman

The woman of amazing character that I have just introduced is the Proverbs 31 woman. I had trouble deciding where to go with this section, as I have spoken so many times on this. Proverbs 31 is one of my favourite passages of scripture. However, I believe that the passage speaks for itself, so I will, as far as possible, refer to it directly throughout.

Apparently, each verse of this section of Proverbs 31 (v10-31) starts with a different letter of the Hebrew alphabet. Perhaps originally Proverbs 31 was used as a memorable poem to help young women?

Some authors state that these verses would make any woman feel inadequate because they cannot match up to the standards of the perfect, wise woman described here. But isn't that the theme of the whole Bible? God sets the standard, raises the bar and then reminds us of our value, which is "far above jewels". He tells us that our value lies not in what we achieve, but in who we are. We serve a God of grace who has set an ideal for us, but when we fall short, He's there to pick us up, dust us off, love us and encourage us to try again.

Let's start towards the end of Proverbs 31 at verse 28: *"Her children rise up and call her blessed; her husband also, he praises* her." In The Message we read, *"Her children respect and bless her; her husband joins in with words of praise."*

Do you want your children (natural or spiritual) to bless you, to respect you? This is a little more than one of those Mother's Day cards with poems about how you're the best mum on the planet. Here, "blessed" is translated as "one who enjoys happy circumstances and whose joy radiates to others".

I would like to be the kind of mother whose joy radiates to my children; the kind of mother who enjoys life with them and they are happy because I am. One of my most simple but most important prayers for my children is that they are happy. What better way is there to encourage this than for me to be happy!

Let's look at a few attributes of this Proverbs 31 woman to help us develop the character traits that will cause our children (natural or spiritual) to rise up and call us blessed.

ATTRIBUTE 1: SHE BRINGS GOOD, NOT HARM

The first character trait of our friend is that she aims to bring good, not harm. Verse 12 says, *"She brings him good, not harm, all the days of her life."*

Firstly, do you believe that you are good? I want to convince you that you are! I constantly tell our girls they are good women. The reason that you are good is that you were created that way!

"So God created man in his own image, in the image of God he created him male and female he created them." (Genesis 1:27)

We all agree that God is good. Therefore, if we are made in His image then we are also good.

In case you are in disagreement, read Genesis 1:31:

"God saw all that he had made, and it was very good."

Nothing God created can be bad – it's impossible, and voices that tell you otherwise are wrong and you should tell them so!

Many of our ministries have the privilege of working with people coming out of prison. It takes time for them to believe that they were created good and that they have just made bad choices.

God still created them good.

Now that we have established that we are good, how can we ensure that we bring good and not harm to our family, friends and the others we do life with? The Message uses the word "generous" to replace "good" used in verse 12. The Amplified version expands the word "good" to "comforts, encourages and does him good."

Most importantly, we can provide a good, healthy environment for our families. One important role of a mother is to protect her children from anything which might harm them and provide them with a good, clean, healthy environment to grow up in. We live in a world that is often not good; to give a child no protection from this is crazy.

I love it how Bobbie Houston puts it in her book *Heaven is in This House*:

"I actually believe that healthy families produce magnificent (splendid, imposing, impressive and excellent) human beings. Not necessarily perfect... but without doubt splendid, imposing, impressive and excellent human beings emerge from environments that are basically healthy. In observing life, one does not generally find such people emerging from broken, neglected, inharmonious or dysfunctional backgrounds. Now that doesn't mean they cannot. The human spirit has the capacity to surface triumphant from the most hideous of situations, but more often than not, negative environments can sadly leave their mark."

As a mother, naturally to my own children and spiritually to the children of my church, I want to do all I can to ensure that they grow up in environments that cause them to be "magnificent".

I believe we can do this by speaking positively about ourselves and them. Things grow well in a healthy, positive environment. My kids recently came home with one of those McDonald's toys – a "Grow Your Own Cress" set. We patiently put the hedgehog shaped plant pot together (that was tricky enough!). Then it was a case of laying the seeds on some paper and watering them – simple, hey? My children were looking forward to lush green cress with their salads in a few days. The trouble is, I put the hedgehog plant pots on the window sill far above the reach of my children. This meant they couldn't see them and thus forgot to water them! The pots were actually hidden behind my chopping board so, for a few days, I also forgot to water them.

What I also forgot when we planted them was that we were due to go away in a few days' time. The poor seeds had now been subject to a drought. They went from a lack of water to being subject to a flood, when I eventually did remember to water them! The poor plants then had to travel several hundred miles by car, sandwiched between the in-car DVD player and my son's bag of books. The cress was then placed upon another window ledge whose owner is slightly more green fingered than me (my mother) and they were watered frequently. However, that poor cress never did enjoy sitting lushly on a salad. It ended up in the bin!

The damage had been done; the cress started off in a negative environment and stood no chance later in life.

We understand that by the grace of God, He has the power to heal the damage caused by negative environments in our lives, but this is no easy or pain free experience. How much better it would be if we provided a healthy, positive environment for our children to grow up in.

Stormie O'Martin in her book, *The Power of a Praying Parent*, says, "Our children's lives don't ever have to be left to chance." She encourages us to pray for them. How true! How often do we hear the parents of a rebellious teenager say that they are praying for their child or they ask friends to pray for their child? But why not start this discipline of praying for your child from a young age?

There are so many things that can harm our children and our families in this fallen world. It is impossible to protect them from all of it, but these verses say, *"She brings them good not harm."* You can most certainly have control over what you bring your family. Good or harm, it's your choice; your responsibility.

ATTRIBUTE 2: SHE PROVIDES
"She gets up while it is still dark: she provides food for her family and portions for her servant girls." (verse 15)

Naturally we understand that we need food to grow. Over the last four years it has been wonderful that James and I have been able to visit two children in Uganda that we sponsor a number of times. I feel so privileged – this is something that most people never get to do once in a lifetime and we have done it four times so far! One thing that has blessed and encouraged us regarding the value of child sponsorship has been seeing the children we sponsor grow. Daniel has grown from a distended bellied, large-eyed, unhappy looking three year old, to a six year old full of life and vitality! He's the same size as my own six year old and academically appears to be doing as well. The provision of food, finance, healthcare, education and love has caused him to grow.

Last summer whilst in Uganda, the little girl we have sponsored more recently contracted malaria. As I held her in my arms she was hot, floppy and listless. I asked the question, "Will she be okay?" I was told that with the correct medical treatment she would be just fine. I found that hard to believe as she looked so ill. I was able to sit and hold her for the afternoon and she dozed in and out of a fever-induced sleep. I was worried she might not pull through, but the next day I was astounded when this little girl came bouncing up to me. I could hardly believe this was the same child; she was full of life and energy. The provision of medical treatment had caused her to be healthy. I was later told that if she hadn't been a sponsored child there would have been no money for medication and she could well have died.

The difference between life and death – that's what provision is.

Let's think about this in the spiritual sense. Food is required for our children to grow in their faith. What are you providing for your children? What activities do you prioritise? Are they ones that will help them grow in their relationship with God and give them good spiritual food or just the ones that all their friends go to? What do you look for in a church? I hope a good Bible-based kids' church is high on any family's list of priorities.

If you are a leader what are you inputting into your kids and youth programmes? What training are you giving your workers?

Please never see kids' church as a babysitting service. Children grow out of the need for a babysitter, but they never grow out of the need for the Word of God.

Provision is way more than natural and spiritual food – it's about what we encourage our children to watch and read, the boundaries we set, the atmosphere in our home.

Our friend, Mrs PR31, not only provided for her family but also for her servant girls. I don't have any servants as such, but I do have some women and some men who serve me in different capacities: my babysitters, our staff at BCC and my fellow leaders. I suppose you could go as far to say my window cleaner, the man who delivers my Tesco order, my hairdresser... how do I provide for these who serve me? Do I carry an atmosphere of provision with me, so that they are blessed when they are with me?

Let's pause for a break here in the attributes of the Proverbs 31 lady. Here I include a story from a mother who recently came to know Jesus. I love this story because it shows how, already, though young in her faith, she has begun to apply these attributes.

How has being a mum changed since I became a Christian?

BY ANITA BATES – FRIEND, NEIGHBOUR & FELLOW BCC'ER

First up, I never thought of myself as a strong woman, nor a good mother. Now, I look back at my journey and realise the changes in me that following God and becoming a Christian has brought to my life – and therefore the influence this has had upon my children. When I reflect on the type of woman and mother I was, there is an amazing contrast with only one contributing factor: I believe that Jesus died on the cross for me to take away my sins and to free me to start my life over again. I am reborn.

As a family we had become very angry with each other. Most women would be embarrassed to admit they were verbally and physically aggressive on a short fuse, both with their husband and children. The reality is, our whole house was affected by conflict, mood swings, arguments and physical fights, all as a result of my attitude at home. This is not a parenting skill to adopt. The children's behaviours were simply copied from those acted out by me.

But Jesus has redeemed me of that sin and, as written in Matthew 11:29-30, I went to God with my burden and asked him to give me rest. I now offer up my prayers and requests to God, give Him thanks for my life and agree to follow the guidelines that He reveals to me in scripture. This has made me stronger and I have developed faith to trust in God to provide me with everything I need to prepare the next generation in His church that we are building and to give me eternal life.

Being a mother at BCC is amazing. You are loved and accepted for who you are and inspired and encouraged to be all that you can be – a philosophy that is mirrored in motherhood in itself: my kids are who they are and I encourage them to flourish. Having great mums and positive women at BCC provides an environment in which women openly support each other and City Pastors listen and guide those who need support.

So, what has changed?

Me and my attitude to life and relationships. When God saved me, and therefore our house, it was with a KABOOM moment, predominantly with scriptures and preaches shouting volumes at me. I actually asked Pastor Becky if she had written a particular preach just for me one week!

There are two things I would like to share with you here as they are relevant to my journey: the scripture that impacted my attitude most dramatically and caused a change in my behaviour, and my "weird moment" with God that affected my relationship with my children in a very poignant way. Firstly, the scripture from Psalm 4:4: *"Don't sin by letting anger control you, think about it overnight and remain silent."*

I'm not saying we live in a silent house now, but we reflect where we need to, regularly forgive each other, and consider how Jesus would have expected us to handle a situation. Secondly, my "weird moment" that I now know to be God telling me, "The time is right Anita, I'm here for you."

A quick bit of background on my relationship with my daughter, so that you fully understand the impact this has had. My daughter was a stroppy, foot stamping Daddy's girl, with very little care for Mummy-cuddles and Mummy in general. On our second visit to a BCC gathering, she grabbed my face with both hands and planted a huge kiss on my lips. I asked her what that was for and she told me that God told her to do it. Thank you God! These kisses are now given of her free will and the cuddles are endless to both Mummy and Daddy.

My children were already attending City Kids before I joined an Alpha course. They are now delighted that Mummy believes in God and our relationship has improved dramatically. We spend so much more time together, regularly praying together, discussing the Bible stories that we are reading and talking about how important God is to us. My oldest child is a worrier and can find some situations quite challenging. A great BCCer mum gave me this scripture and now my son repeats it when troubled. I hope you find it useful too: *"We can do all things through Christ who gives us strength"* (Philippians 4:13).

My children realise that not everyone believes in God and that some people worship other gods, but they genuinely believe that our God is the best! #PRAISE!

ATTRIBUTE 3: SHE WORKS HARD

Verse 17 is interesting because the NIV states, *"She sets about her work vigorously."* The NKJV says, *"She girds herself with strength."* The Amplified verdion is similar and The Message puts it in plain English: *"First thing in the morning, she dresses for work, rolls up her sleeves, eager to get started."* It's easy to see that she is a hard worker.

I used to work with a guy who, every morning, would walk into the office and say, "Mother, if you love me burn my working clothes!" This did amuse me because he lived at home with his mother. I think he dropped the swear word that some of you may realise was originally in this saying, for my benefit. He would then plod through his working day. I was on placement as a student Town Planner, working hard to learn all I could to qualify as a Chartered Town Planner. He, on the other hand, seemed content to handle menial tasks with little ambition for promotion or bettering himself. At the end of each working day, dead on 5pm, you'd hear a huge sigh as he got up from his desk and said, "Another day another dollar." As amused as I was by this gentleman, I was actually very sad that this was his existence and attitude to life. It is the opposite attitude to our wife of noble character who appears to be "up and at 'em". Being hard working is a good character trait to develop. Just look at a few of the warnings throughout scripture about laziness:

"Lazy hands make a poor man [or woman] *but diligent hands bring wealth."* (Proverbs 10:4)

"If a man [or woman] *is lazy, the rafters sag; if his hands are idle, the house leaks."* (Ecclesiastes 10:18)

Have you ever noticed the "household" with the rafters sagging and the house leaking? I don't mean literally – although I'm sure we all know a few of those too! I mean the people whose lives seem to be falling apart. Nothing goes right for them; they live in utter chaos. Could it be that they are not working vigorously? That they refuse to roll their sleeves up?

This woman didn't just work hard for the sake of working hard, her hard work was profitable. Proverbs 14:23 says, *"All hard work brings a profit."* A profit is a return for your work. The farmer sows his seed with the expectation of a crop. The business man invests his money with the anticipation of a return. Is your hard work bringing a profit? Be wise when making judgement on this statement, because sometimes a profit is not seen immediately – the business world calls it a long term investment. Christians often call it, "God are you ever going to show up?"

I am a very simple person really and recently I have made some very simple decisions when considering this equation: hard work = profit. With my first two children I used real nappies because it worked out more economical. I also liked the idea of being environmentally friendly and there's nothing more cute than a clean baby in a snug (clean) real nappy. I sold my real nappies, however, and now with my third child approaching I have been considering the following equation (I told you I was simple!): washing nappies alongside a family of five's washing + working full time + the expense of buying real nappies for one child equates to a formula that looks like this:

mess + hard work = stress and not much profit

I have made a monumental decision. Pampers here I come!

You may laugh, but sometimes we create work for ourselves that really brings no profit. Please try applying this principle to your life as a whole, not just to nappies!

It also seems that the PR31 woman took responsibility for her work. Verse 18 says, *"Her lamp does not go out at night."* How I hate the phrase, "It's not my responsibility" in church life!

Hang on, was the Great Commission addressed to us all?

Does the "body" just mean some of us?

A lost and dying generation is the responsibility of all of us.

Did I walk past that person on Sunday because it's the Welcome Team's responsibility to shake their hand?

Did I fail to pick up that piece of litter in the car park because the Cleaning Team does that?

Did I decide not to give a hug to the young lady who looked upset because the Pastoral Team should be doing that?

We've all done it!

At BCC we have banned the word "rota" because it comes with the stereotypical idea that "one week I'm responsible and the next week I'm not". Instead, we encourage teams to share and take responsibility. The old saying goes, "A bit of hard work never hurt anyone." How true! Especially when there's a dying generation to be reached!

ATTRIBUTE 4: SHE CARES FOR THE POOR AND NEEDY

Verse 20 of Proverbs 31 describes a woman who *"opens her arms to the poor and extends her hands to the needy."*

As the Church, we have been clearly mandated to care for the orphan and the widow. James 1:27 (NIV) says, *"Religion that God our Father accepts as pure and faultless is this: to look after orphans and widows in their distress..."*

But this is so much more than a burden or a duty for us as Christians or as the Church – this is actually the heart of God. I love Psalm 68:5-6 (NIV):

"Father to the fatherless, a defender of widows, is God in his holy dwelling. God sets the lonely in families; he leads forth the prisoners with singing..."

I had a short period of my life where I wasn't physically living in a family. Whilst I was at university I can remember the loneliness that I experienced at times after coming from a loving family environment. Then I got married and had children of my own and once again, for the last 12 years, I have been part of a family.

That place where we call home, we feel safe and loved. However, this is not everybody's experience. Some may, for whatever reason, have had to leave their natural family and they now find themselves an "orphan". For some, this separation has been a choice to remove themselves from an abusive situation perhaps or from a lifestyle that is not helpful. Others may have found themselves in this situation unexpectedly, perhaps because of the sudden death of parents or because they have been forced to leave their home environment. We can have such stereotypical image of an "orphan" or a "widow" that we sometimes fail to recognise them in our church or community. It is impressed upon me that, as the Church, we need to continue to pursue this cause. That means you and me as individual Christians. This is our cause that we can all play a part in.

On several occasions, when booking young women into BCC's residential facility for vulnerable young women, we have come to complete the "next of kin" form and girls have told me, "I don't know what to write." Initially I had thought they didn't understand the term "next of kin", but actually it has been because they don't have a next of kin. There is no one who will care if they are ill; no one who's even bothered if they are dead or alive!

Yes, really, this is happening in 21st Century Britain!

As a mother myself this breaks my heart, because my love for my children, as with most mothers, is so strong that if one of my children were ill I would travel from the other side of the world as quickly as I could to get to them. If that is my heart, imagine God's heart whose love is perfect. This, I believe, is why He calls the Church to rise up and be a father to the fatherless, a mother to the motherless, a defender of widows and a family to the orphan. What a privilege that God would entrust His precious children to us, the Church!

I believe we can all do something; we can invite that person for lunch, we can take them shopping, we can give them a hug, we can give them time, we can open our family doors at Christmastime and we can make a fuss of them on their birthday... and so much more.

I have witnessed so many BCCers who act out this heartbeat of God: the mentor who told me she always gives her mentee a hug when they meet "because there is no one else who will hug her"; the families who invite those not in families to Christmas lunch; the City Pastors who visit those in hospital who would otherwise have no visitors; the Embrace team member who makes a fuss of someone who perhaps hasn't seen a friendly face for days; the BCCer who travels halfway across the city to pick someone up for church.

The list goes on.

As a leader I will ensure our church always extends its hand to the poor and needy. As a mother, I will endeavour to ensure my family does the same.

ATTRIBUTE 5: SHE CLOTHES HERSELF WITH STRENGTH AND DIGNITY

Verse 25 says, *"She clothes herself with strength and dignity."*

I recently attended a Colour Me Beautiful session. The idea is that according to your natural hair, eye and skin colourings you are given a set of colours for clothing that will make you look your best. It was an interesting exercise and as soon as I am out of maternity clothes, which you don't get a huge colour choice in, I shall be applying what I learnt and adjusting my wardrobe accordingly.

These colours are supposed to make me look my best and I am sure they will help, but I like the sound of being clothed in strength and dignity. To me that sounds like a colour palette that Colour Me Beautiful can't provide!

I have already written a lot about strength throughout this book, but what about dignity? How do we clothe ourselves in dignity? Having studied the meaning of the word, I wonder if it is more about our mindset than anything else? I think it is more probable that a person who understands their value will have dignity.

She clothes herself with strength and dignity

Last year I spoke about this at a ladies' conference in Uganda. It broke my heart that the women there couldn't look me in the eye as I spoke about their value. I asked them to repeat after me, "I am valuable" and the response was laughter. I was so shocked I asked my interpreter, the pastor's wife, why they were laughing. She explained that they were embarrassed because no one had ever told them they were valued. I could have wept. I explained to them that Proverbs 31 compares their worth to "far above jewels" or "more than many rubies".

I went on to explain that a street prostitute and the Queen of England have the same value in God's eyes – that these women had the same value in God's eyes as our ladies back at BCC. Their lives may be very different, but their value is the same. Their value was not wrapped up in their position, their value was *them*. I encouraged them to lift their heads up! I told them that they ARE fearfully and wonderfully made. As I watched the faces lift up towards me, I began to see something very beautiful: women clothed with dignity!

In the natural these women know how to dress with dignity far better than we do. You never see a revealing t-shirt or a skirt a bit too short. They are dignified in the way they honour others. The mother of the little girl we sponsor met me on bended knees with tears of thankfulness in her eyes. What a dignified way to express gratitude. My prayer is that they remember, as we should, that they are valued.

We have the tag line on all our material for women, "Her worth is far above jewels" because I want women to believe it. Engraved on our graduation necklaces for Stronger is, "Far above jewels". I want girls to remember it.

ATTRIBUTE 6: SHE SPEAKS WITH WISDOM

"She speaks with wisdom and faithful instruction is on her lips" (verse 26)

I feel very inadequate when people ask me for my wisdom on a subject. I feel inadequate writing this book; what do I know?

Yet, I know that wisdom is something that we should pursue and develop in our lives. It is wisdom that helps us make right decisions; wisdom that keeps us on track when things are tough; wisdom that provides the answer your child needs; wisdom that enables you to break through a seemingly unsolvable problem.

I was challenged recently when a visiting speaker came and spoke to our leaders. He gave a warning to our girls from Proverbs 14:1 which reads, *"The wise woman builds her house, but with her own hands the foolish one tears hers down."*

His point was this: that the wise and the foolish woman could be one and the same person! How true! How easy to one day be full of wisdom, on top of the world, and the next be so down in the dumps you couldn't care less about the disaster you could cause with your actions.

This I believe is a wise and timely warning to us as women, especially if we are struggling with being controlled by our emotions. We should never act out of emotion, but from a place of wisdom based in God's Word.

Oh, how we need wisdom as leaders and wisdom as mothers! Leadership can throw us into some pretty interesting situations which often we've had no training to deal with! It's God's anointing and His wisdom that will help us deal with these situations in a way that builds up and does not tear down; that restores and heals and causes the much needed breakthrough.

As mothers we must be aware that our children will face issues that we have never had to deal with. Life is different to how it was when we were kids. We live in an increasingly corrupt world. We will need to answer questions that naturally we do not have the answers to.

Perhaps your child has a totally different character to you and you cannot understand where he/she is coming from? You will need wisdom in helping them. Perhaps a spiritual child has been through situations you cannot even comprehend; they are desperate and need help. Naturally speaking, you will be flummoxed for answers. Only God's wisdom will help you to help that individual.

Wisdom apparently comes with old age, but wisdom is not just for the aged:

"Get wisdom, get understanding; do not forget my words or swerve from them. Do not forsake wisdom, and she will protect you; love her, and she will watch over you. Wisdom is supreme; therefore get wisdom. Though it cost all you have, get understanding." (Proverbs 4:5-7)

I think we all understand where wisdom comes from. Perhaps we just need to read God's Word more and apply it.

There is so much more we could glean from our friend in Proverbs 31 and I am sure, like me, you will benefit visiting her regularly to help you hone and define your character. I now want to move on to look at another woman of strength and compare her to some "cowards" who serve as warnings to us.

CHAPTER 5

5 Cowards & A Strong Woman

Whilst in Uganda last year, myself and BCC's Social Action Stream Pastor ended up stuck in a minibus alone for about eight hours with a Ugandan driver who spoke little English. It was a random trip that should only have taken two hours each way, but the driver, in his wisdom, decided it would be a good idea to go via the city centre, Kampala, to book a table for our team's evening meal. I did offer him my phone to make the reservation, however I'm not sure he understood.

So we endured a four hours each way trip instead! This gave us plenty of time to chat and we ended up sharing life stories. As I told Jo about my family and some of my life experiences she commented, "Wow! So you come from a heritage of strong women." I have since pondered this and have to agree that I am fortunate to have a family lineage of some remarkably strong women who I am proud to call my relatives. In fact, thinking about it, the Croome family (my maiden name) is renowned for its strong women.

Grandma Croome was a woman of strength herself. While her husband was at war she bore a child and although very poorly, she battled through and continued to head up a "moving and shaking" Scout movement in South Wales. She was a tower of strength to both her first born and my father and nothing fazed her. Having no daughters herself I am sure she was delighted to have five granddaughters – all of whom carry that Croome trait of strength. The eldest set up a drop-in centre for the homeless in Manchester Cathedral, a truly inspiring project. Then comes me – you can make your own judgements on that one! My sister will hate me saying this but, as a single mother, she does the most outstanding job of managing a teaching job, maintaining a home and bringing up her daughter. Then we have the youngest two who had an interesting and unconventional upbringing: one has recently come to faith, realising that only God could provide her healing. She and her husband are now involved in church planting. The youngest Croome grandchild is a beautiful young lady who has just achieved a first class honours degree from Bristol University.

When Grandma Croome's husband, my wonderful Grandpa, died early one Christmas Day morning, she handled his death with strength and dignity. I remember her taking the call from the hospital. She was amazingly calm, considering the man she had lived with and loved for the last 70 years had just died. She remained strong through the months that followed and I would often visit her, now she was alone in her house, and offer to help or stay over to keep her company.

Not once did she display any sign of weakness.

Early in my 20's I had a prophecy over my life from Psalm 7:14: *"Wait for the Lord, take heart be strong and wait for the Lord."*

At the time I needed patience, but little did I realise the

strength I would need in the years to come as I journeyed through this life we call leadership. Although I may come from a line of strong women, I do not believe that strength is hereditary. You have to work to develop it.

So in this section, let me focus now particularly on the importance of strength. Firstly, I want to address five "cowards" who didn't display this all-important character trait. If you are a male reading this book, please don't be offended that all the cowards are men! This is purely coincidental and I am sure there is many a woman who struggles with the same traps as these men of the Bible did!

PETER: THE TRAP OF FEAR

Peter is an interesting character in the Bible. His name is changed from Simon, meaning "hearer", to Peter, meaning "rock". Quite a significant character shift and, of course, what's more important is that it was Jesus who changed his name. This says to me that Jesus believed in Peter. He believed he would be a rock. We know the story of Peter and we know that his character transformation, though it had been declared in word through his name change, had yet to be outworked and learnt by Peter himself.

Sometimes we can get so discouraged when we read what God believes of us in the Bible. We step back and look at our lives and think, "Really? Me? I don't think so!" Remember, we are all a work in progress! Yes, it's what Jesus calls us to be; yes, it might take some hard work to get there – but be encouraged, God believes you can get there otherwise He wouldn't have said it!

Jesus describes Peter not as who he is, but who he will

become and He does the same for you! Peter, on his journey of becoming "rock", faced some challenges. One of those was the trap of fear – a challenge that can trap any one of us.

In John 13 we see Jesus predict Peter's denial – or predict the trap he will fall into.

John 13:38 says, *"Will you really lay down your life for me? I tell you the truth, before the cock crows, you will disown me three times."*

Ouch! In Matthew 26:35 we see Peter's response: *"Even if I have to die with you, I will never disown you."*

Now, let's not be too judgemental towards Peter. What about us? We sing the songs on a Sunday morning, "I am yours ... I will follow you ... I live for you ... there is none besides you ... you are all I need."

Then comes Monday morning and our faith starts to shake...

By Tuesday we've forgotten that God is on the throne of our lives...

By Thursday it's all gone to pot and we're looking to see what the horoscope says about our lives...

By Saturday we feel so condemned that we know we need to get to church on Sunday to put it all right!

To read John 18:17-18 and John 18:25-27 is painful. It's like one of the movies you watch where you are on the edge of your seat, begging the character, "Don't do it! You're making the wrong decision!"

Then of course they do it and you're saying, "Why did you have to go and do that? How stupid – now the movie is ruined!" We are not talking once, not twice but three times! Surely at some point Peter must have thought, "Doh! I'm doing that thing

Jesus said I was going to. Stop! I don't want to do it!" But he didn't and he didn't for the same reason as us: we can often make repeated mistakes out of fear! Three times Peter was a coward. He failed to acknowledge that Jesus was His Lord, because of fear.

Don't fall for the "Peter trap" of fear! Don't trade strength for fear because only cowards are fearful.

Psalm 23:4 says, *"Even though I walk through the valley of the shadow of death, I will fear no evil..."*

Even in the darkest of situations we do not need to fear!

Psalm 46: 1-2:

"God is our refuge and strength... therefore we will not fear."

Peter was scared about what might happen if he owned up to being a follower of Jesus. Perhaps he would get arrested too? Perhaps he'd be put to death? To put this in context, Peter was a husband and a father.

What about you? Will you fall into the trap of fear? Or will you stand firm on God's Word?

PILATE: THE TRAP OF SELF-PRESERVATION

Pilate was the Roman procurator at the time of Jesus' arrest and crucifixion. He was an interesting character because he didn't fall into the trap easily. It's clear from the story told in John 18 and 19 that he wrestled with the decision to crucify Jesus. In the end he made the wrong decision and legend has it that Pilate ended up committing suicide. He knew he'd done wrong and couldn't live with himself.

Let's look at this trap of self-preservation because any one of us could so easily trade in the character trait of strength for it.

Firstly, in John 18:31 we find Pilate trying to avoid making a decision: *"Take him yourselves and judge him by your own way."*

If you are a leader you cannot hide from tough decisions!

In John 18:33 we see Pilate, hoping to find a reason to crucify Jesus, talking to him privately, asking, *"Are you the King of the Jews?"*

Self-preservation will always try and cast the blame elsewhere.

By verse 38 I think Pilate is desperately battling with his conscience: *"What is truth?"* Once again he lays the decision-making burden on someone else's head and infers to the people that Jesus isn't guilty, asking them, *"Do you want me to release 'the King of the Jews'?"*

As a leader, don't succumb to people pleasing. It will get you nowhere fast!

In John 19:4 we once again see Pilate fall in the trap of self-preservation: *"I find no basis for a charge against him."*

Why let it happen then? Come on, Pilate, stand up and be a man! Be a leader! He was the Governor! He could have put a stop to this!

"Pilate was even more afraid" (John 19:8). Of course he was and we should always be afraid when we know we are making a decision based on self-preservation rather than God's will.

By verse 12 we see Pilate realising he's made the wrong decision and trying to set Jesus free. By verse 14 he acknowledges him as king but still refuses to stand up for him.

He knew that if he stood up to the Jews he may risk his job! Caesar could have said he was supporting rebels who believed Jesus was king rather than himself. Pilate was in a position of power. He had a title and presumably a nice life and a good pay package to go with it. If he were to go against the wishes of the people would he be hated rather than respected? What about Caesar, his boss? What would he do if Pilate went against the people's choice? Could he lose his job?

So to preserve himself and his title he took the coward's way! How easy to think this could never happen to us, but I'm sure that, if we are honest, it has and does! We need to develop strength so that we do not take the coward's way.

JOSEPH OF ARIMEATHEA: THE TRAP OF THE SECRET

"Later, Joseph of Arimeathea asked Pilate for the body of Jesus. Now Joseph was a disciple of Jesus, but secretly because he feared the Jews." (John 19: 38)

This is interesting! I have included Joseph of Arimeathea in my rogues' gallery of cowards for the one single sentence above. How can you be a disciple of Jesus "in secret"? This baffles me!

The English Dictionary defines a "disciple" as:

1. A follower of the doctrines of a teacher or a school of thought
2. One of the personal followers of Christ (including his 12 apostles) during His earthly life.

How can you be a follower in secret? How would someone not notice your behaviours, your views, mindsets and opinions? Apparently it would have been difficult for Joseph to be a follower of Jesus publicly because he was a member of the Sanhedrin.

"Apparently" it may be difficult for you to be a follower of Jesus in your workplace, college, school or family.

Really?

Or maybe, just maybe, you have been placed there by God to bring hope and light to lost and dying people?

I used to work in a pub as a student during my summer holidays. Being a particular public house chain that sold low cost beer, it was a pub for "drinkers". As much as they tried to glamorise it and make it a family pub, the bottom line was it would attract people who were after cheap beer and lots of it.

I loved this job because of the type of people I used to meet. I worked the 11 till 7 shift when the pub was generally quiet, except for the office workers' lunch break and I had time to chat to the regulars.

There were several older gentlemen who I became very fond of. There was one who used to come in and say, "Rebecca, fill that glass to the top. That's right, push it all down and make the bottom bowed." Then there was Mr. Kronenbourg, as we called him. In those days Kronenbourg was £1.76 a pint (unbelievable, right?) He would have the exact change every time and he would neatly stack it on the bar ready for me, then return in half an hour and do the same, and again, and again!

These men seemed to have little else going on in their lives and on occasion I would have the opportunity to tell them about church or Jesus.

None of them ever got down from their bar stool and confessed the sinner's prayer, but I could not imagine in that situation keeping my faith a secret. These people needed Jesus more than anyone I'd ever met!

Twenty years on from that summer job I had a Facebook message from a former colleague who had tracked me down. He sent me a message saying, "It's great to see you are living out what you talked about all those years ago." He doesn't know Jesus personally, as far as I'm aware, but he certainly knows something of Him because I decided not to fall into the trap of the secret.

Being a Christian in secret doesn't work! You will end up a coward. Joseph appears on the scene after the action, unable to help or support Jesus. The verse I opened with starts with the word "Later". Don't leave it until later to acknowledge Jesus. Don't leave it until later before your friends and work colleagues know you're a Christian.

NICODEMUS: THE TRAP OF WEALTH

When I first preached on this subject to our women I had only four cowards, but after re-reading this section of John's Gospel I found another! He was lurking quietly behind Joseph of Arimeathea.

Cowards often hide!

This may be slightly tenuous and but I wonder if Nicodemus was trapped by his wealth?

John 19:39 says, *"He was accompanied by Nicodemus, the man who earlier visited Jesus at night. Nicodemus brought a mixture of myrrh and aloes, about seventy five pounds."*

Like Joseph of Arimeathea, Nicodemus was obviously an intelligent and influential man. Back in John 3 it was he who came and asked Jesus at night about the meaning of being born again. It's interesting that he came at night. Again, maybe a sign of his cowardice. Later in John 7:51-52 we see Nicodemus trying to stand up for Jesus, but his stand is quashed by the other Pharisees.

Nicodemus could have also been subject to the trap of self-preservation. He, like Pilate, held a position that perhaps he wanted to preserve. But what I find interesting is that, in the end, he was found behind the scenes with Joseph splashing the cash!

From my experience of leading church I am well aware, as you may be, that the trap of wealth produces guilt. The fear of losing money can cause someone to act in a cowardly manner. Then the guilt of holding onto money creeps up on them and this further cripples and prevents them from being generous.

Myrrh and aloes weighing seventy-five pounds represented a very large amount of money. It was on a par with what was spent on royal burials. You may disagree with me here, but bear with me. This was a generous gift, but I wonder whether Nicodemus spent this huge amount of money on Jesus' burial because he was stuck in the trap of wealth and guilt?

The Bible says it's difficult for a rich man to enter the kingdom of Heaven (Matthew 19:23) so we need to understand that the trap of wealth is a serious trap that we need to address.

I believe the beginning of avoiding this trap is the biblical discipline of tithing.

By tithing we are saying, "God, it's all yours anyway."

I feel for people who get saved later in life and have to begin the practice of tithing from a healthy salary.

I am so glad I began tithing from my 50p pocket money as a child and have done so throughout my life. Now when examining our personal finances, that tithe looks a little larger than it did from my 50p pocket money, but I would never consider, as part of a money-saving exercise, reducing or stopping my tithe, no matter how hard times were. It's my first step in ensuring I do not fall into the trap of wealth.

THOMAS: THE TRAP OF LACK OF FAITH

I think Thomas is one of the much loved Bible characters – probably because we can all identify with him to some degree!

We find his story in John 20:24-25. Thomas was one of the disciples and along with the other disciples he would have lived and breathed with Jesus. No doubt the disciples would have been good friends, having travelled, witnessed many miracles and faced many challenges together. These kinds of life experiences draw you close as friends and form a common bond and trust. Why then would he feel the need to question his friends, the other disciples, when they reported to him that they had seen Jesus? In fact, he more than questioned it, he flatly refused to believe it unless he saw if for himself!

The consequence of Thomas' unbelief was that he went a week not believing that Jesus had risen. A full week later, Jesus, full of grace, appears to him, but condemns him and commends those who believe without seeing. That's called faith!

Jesus says to Thomas and, I believe, says to us, *"Stop doubting and believe"* (verse 27).

The trap of lack of faith is so debilitating. It can cause us to fail to move into all God has for us. You may need to stand in faith for finances, for resources, for decisions, for fears or a whole host of other things. Stop doubting and believe!

When we came to BCC there were a handful of women who all desired to become pregnant. They had prayed and nothing was happening. During one particular pre-service prayer meeting we decided as leaders to stand in faith over this issue. We declared the promises of God and stood together spiritually with these women. Sure enough, within a few months we began to hear of one pregnancy after another and another. One lady even received a double blessing of twins.

People talk of the "leap of faith" referring to those mad people who jump off tall buildings or out of aeroplanes. Their head tells them that they will be fine because they know the parachute or rope has been tried and tested, but their heart, I would imagine, is telling them, "Don't do it – there could have been a mistake!"

Well God doesn't make mistakes!

His rope or parachute won't fail – so what are you waiting for?

THE STRONG WOMAN – MARY

I opened this chapter by saying please pay no attention to the fact we have described five males as cowards. Now we look at a female character of strength! Of course, Peter, our first coward went on to become a man of great strength – proving that a coward can move past the traps and become all God has called them to be. Hebrews 11 lists a whole host of other characters of strength. I have just happened to focus on Mary as she jumped out at me after reading through John's Gospel.

She appears just after the five cowards we have explored. What I noticed was the character differences between her and them. The story I am referring to is found in John 20: 11-18 and starts with the words, *"BUT Mary..."* The disciples have gone home but Mary remains at the tomb. She is different, already standing out from the crowd.

If wonder if God can say about me, "BUT Becky..."?

My Bible notes say that Jesus appeared to Mary first because she needed Him the most, maybe because she was the weaker sex or maybe because of her previous life issues? I disagree! I think Mary's life had been changed the most and she had the bigger understanding of God. Perhaps she loved Jesus the most? In Luke 8:2 we learn that Jesus had driven seven evil spirits out of her. She knew what it was to live in the lost, lonely and tormented state without Jesus, and she knew what it was to live alongside Jesus as her Lord and Saviour.

So let's look at some of her character traits that show she wasn't a coward. Perhaps we can apply them to our own lives to enable us to step into being that strong woman of God I believe you and I are called to be.

DECLARE

Firstly, she publicly declares Jesus as "My Lord" in John 20:13. She was crying. The more accurate translation says "wailing". I'm not sure she was in any fit state to see who was asking her the question. But whoever it was, she was willing to publicly say without fear or hesitation that Christ was her Lord.

A woman of strength is able to publicly state that Jesus is her Lord, in charge, the boss of her life.

SACRIFICE

Secondly, she was willing to pay the cost. In verse 15 we discover Mary thinks it's the gardener talking to her and she asks, *"Sir, if you have carried him away, tell me where you have put him and I will go and get him."*

OK, now think this through: a fully grown man, dead, weighs a fair weight and her plan was to go and get him. She was alone, the disciples had gone home. How exactly did she think she was going to pull this one off? How far was she imagining that she was going to have to carry Him, alone!

I don't think these thoughts even entered her head – she loved Jesus. She loved to serve Him and she was willing to pay the price.

Our staff team at BCC amaze me with the cost they are willing to pay, often in a very personal way, because of their heart for God and their church.

OBEDIENCE

Another strength of Mary's was that she was obedient. In verse 17 we see Jesus' request that she goes to tell the disciples and in verse 18 she goes to do just that, no questions asked. I'm not sure about you, but I think I would have liked a cup of tea and a chat with Jesus first to find out all the details. What happened? Where have you been? Are you okay? What's going to happen now? These are the same questions I can find myself asking Jesus when He asks me to do something! Perhaps I should learn from Mary and just do as I'm told. Perhaps her faith and trust in God Almighty was so great, she didn't need to question.

DEVOTED

Lastly, and this one really gets me, Mary was devoted. Mary was the last at the cross and the first at the grave. She stood at the cross whilst most of the disciples were hiding. She got up early, alone, to go to His grave to serve Him however she could. Is Jesus your first and your last? Mary broke all the rules, she travelled with Jesus (women weren't meant to do that), she went on a seven day walk to follow Him, she gave her time and finances to Jesus. I believe she knew that, without Jesus, she was nothing. She knew her strength was found in Him.

I feel challenged by this wonderful woman of God. I hope you too are able to take something from her life and apply it to your own.

I hope this section has encouraged you regarding the importance of character. At BCC we often say, "Who you are is so much more important than what you do." How can you do without first being? Doing is only based on your being.

Character takes a lifetime to develop, but I love the fact that we have a plumb line to work to. I continue to look to my friend in Proverbs 31 and adjust my life accordingly – to aim to become that rare woman that is hard to find. Women, let's stand together in this pursuit, so that we can all shout from our church doors, "We're all in here!" Let me finish with the story of a fellow leader who has taken up the challenge of character.

Being a Leader and a Mother
BY SARA JUKES – EXECUTIVE PASTOR

Foundationally, for me being a leader and a mother, is the fact that "I am a leader" and "I am a mother" – each is part of the outworking of who I am and it is essential that each of these aspects live in harmony with each other.

At BCC we believe who you are is more important than what you do. Often, as women, what we do is a greatly interwoven part of who we are. It is an outworking of the "who". Therefore, in a leadership capacity, knowing the "who" is essential, so that the "what" is done out of personal unity, strength and intent, not internal battle, emotion and reaction.

I am intentional about being a mum and a leader. It's a journey of growing in capacity, putting God first and not making excuses.

"Seek the Kingdom of God above all else, and live righteously, and he will give you everything you need." (Matthew 6:33)

I learnt the first lesson early on, that God is ultimately in control, knowing and seeing everything for you and your children. My first child, Grace, was breech. I was desperate for a natural birth but had to have a C-section after we found she had a true knot in her umbilical cord and a natural birth could have been fatal. God knew best and Grace is a healthy six-year old.

During my pregnancy with our second child, Olivia, we had not long been on the BCC journey and I was conscious that it was important for me to model this well as a mother and leader. I was fully aware this was not a time for excuses, but a time for stepping up and setting an example to help others who followed on the same journey.

My girls are so important to me; I would lay my life down for them and God is my first love because I know He loves Grace and Liv more than I do. I have peace that in living my life as a leader, God in turn will bless, protect and encourage them through, at times, the sacrifices I make for Him.

Let me put it a different way... One evening when both girls were asleep and I was ironing and praying, I had such a sense of God speaking into my spirit, "If you don't break through then they will have to." To me, that's fighting talk!

I am passionate about the next generation. I am passionate about passing on an awesome church to my girls. I am passionate that in their lives they will be able to stand on the shoulders of giants and therefore reach higher and do more for God than I ever could.

The second thing I have learnt is that we are all about building for future, not the immediate; for the next generation.

So, practically speaking, what can I say to you? Set your face like flint, keep pushing in. It is not about what you are doing, it is about who you are.

Finally, some perspective: the woman in Proverbs 31 was a mum, an entrepreneur, a wife, a trader, a mistress to her servants, a vineyard owner, a seamstress, a good Samaritan and the list goes on ... and her children *"arise and call her blessed"* (Proverbs 31:28).

PART 3:

Leadership

Introduction

On this journey of becoming a strong woman there may be a call of some degree to leadership. Those of us in church circles often think of the leader as the one who stands at the front and preaches, but could I encourage you to understand that leadership comes in many forms: leadership in the House of God, leadership in the home, the family, social settings, the workplace, political settings. My personal calling is to leadership in the House of God, so it is from that angle that I will be writing. However, I hope that the principles discussed will be applicable to leadership elsewhere and at whatever level.

The story of Deborah in Judges 4 and 5 first caught my attention when I read Judges 5:7, which identifies her as, *"Deborah... a mother in Israel."* Having already read chapter 4, I had deduced from her actions that she was also a leader. So here, I thought to myself, we have a mother *and* a leader. Since both these are things that I aspire to do well, I decided that the story of Deborah needed some more unpacking. I hope you agree.

The book of Judges in which Deborah's story is set contains story after story of judges coming to rule as the people keep turning away from God. The role of the judges is described in Judges 2:16: *"The Lord raised up Judges who saved them out of the hands of these raiders..."* and *"...he was with the judge and saved them out of the hands of their enemies as long as the judge lived"* (Judges 2:18). The judges were saviours and also deliverers. The first Judge to be mentioned is Othneil in Judges 3:10, which says, *"The Spirit of the Lord came upon him ... and he went out to war."* They were leaders who were willing to get their hands dirty.

Deborah is the only female who is raised up throughout the book and, alongside Jael, who cunningly and single-handedly takes out Sisera (the captain of the army of Jabin the king) with a tent peg as we see a story unfold. In an anti-female culture, two women most definitely take the lead – not in a domestic environment like Ruth and Naomi, but in a national and political arena. Not only do they take the lead, but they achieve victory over the Canaanites which previous generations had been unable to do.

Bible scholars argue whether Deborah was actually a mother in the natural sense, but my argument is that she considered herself a mother. I believe that God has placed in the heart of every woman the ability and desire to be a mother. I encourage our women, whether they are natural mothers or not, to be mothers! There are so many ways we can be a mother and have a mother's heart. And if Deborah was not a natural mother, I believe that she understood this.

Let's look at the qualities of this strong woman, a leader and a mother.

CHAPTER 6

Deborah

QUALITY 1: INTIMACY

We first hear of Deborah in Judges 4:4: *"Deborah, a prophetess..."* The English dictionary defines the word prophetess as, "A person who supposedly speaks by divine inspiration, especially one through whom a divinity expresses his will."

It's the first thing we hear about Deborah – that she was a prophetess. To me this says that she was known for her closeness to God. People knew she heard from God; people knew that she had a close relationship with Him.

Maybe it was this closeness to God that caused Barak in Judges 4:8 to want Deborah's presence in the battle. Deborah had heard from God. The Israelites were to overthrow Sisera. She called for Barak, who I assume was some kind of chief within the army (he was in charge of 10,000 men so must have held a high rank). Deborah commands him, in God's name, to go to battle against Sisera. Barak's immediate response is, *"If you go with me, I will go; but if you don't go with me, I won't go"* (Judges 4:8).

I don't know about you, but I always feel safe in the presence of mighty men and women of God and I think it was Deborah's closeness to God that Barak was seeking to accompany him on this journey that would be somewhat challenging and hair raising. In case you hadn't noticed, life is challenging and hair raising! I am yet to meet anyone who has a simple, uncomplicated, unchallenging, smooth and easy ride of a life! To know the presence of God as we walk through life is a comfort, a security and a strength to us.

I find it interesting that Deborah's name means "bee", as in the buzzy bee that makes honey. Throughout the Bible names always carry significance, so I feel it's important to look into the meaning of Deborah's name.

Bees are interesting insects, commonly known for their ability to make honey and their ability to sting. In my opinion, I can tolerate bees more than wasps. Wasps appear to have little purpose other than to give you a painful sting. On a recent trip to a country park my son was stung three times by wasps. It was painful, annoying and required medication to be administered. Bees are not known as "busy bees" for no reason. Bees are key in the pollination of plants. Apparently, they focus on collecting either pollen or nectar depending on demand.

I was amazed to discover that it is estimated that one third of the human food supply depends on insect pollination, most of which is accomplished by bees. It is amazing that such a small insect carries such a vital role.

I used to read a book to my boys when they were little called *Buzzy Bee*. It was one of those rhyming stories that starts, "Buzzy Bee is busy, he visits every flower. Working hard from dawn to dusk..." The rest of the rhyme has escaped my memory! However, the essence of the story was that bees are hardworking, productive creatures.

Bear with me, there is a point here! Deborah was named after a bee! It evokes a picture of a woman who is busy and productive. The reason I like this so much is that it lays to rest the misapprehension in Christian circles that anyone who desires to be a "prophet" or wants to hear from God on a regular basis needs to spend all their time basking before Him in meditative prayer and actually doing nothing! Excuse me for being slightly ferocious; in my earlier days of ministry I was slightly more hard faced with what I called the "super spiritual". My stance was: you pray and seek God, I'll go and reach young people for Jesus. Now, of course, my understanding has increased and I am aware that we all need to spend time in the presence of God if we are to be effective for Him.

In our early days of repurposing what is now Breathe City Church (my husband has written an excellent book about this journey called *From Beach Hut To Palace*), a leader was asked to serve on the cafe bar during a day-long event. Her answer was, "It's not my gifting – my gifting is to pray and seek the Lord." I agree that some people have a wonderful gifting and grace to pray and intercede and I am forever grateful for those I know who have done this over mine and James' life – Rosa Warrilow's intercession was key in us making the journey to Stoke on Trent. And there are other prayer warriors, I am sure, without whose intercession for BCC, James and myself would not be where we are today.

However, we are all called to serve! Jesus Himself came to serve. He busied Himself in the business of feeding the hungry, healing the sick and reaching the lost, as well as seeking the will of His Father.

I believe it was through Deborah's "busy bee" character that she became close to God. It was through her servant attitude and her willingness to serve in the House of God. Some reports say that actually, *Lappidoth*, meaning "lamp" or "illuminations", wasn't Deborah's husband, but Judges 4:4 would more accurately be translated as "the woman of Lappidoth":

"Deborah, a prophetess, the wife of Lappidoth, was leading Israel at that time."

Some have taken this to mean that she undertook the servant-hearted menial task of looking after the wicks of the lamps in the temple.

I love this because it does away with the melancholic, "Let's all just pray and seek the Lord until He returns!"

No!

Let's all work hard and seek the Lord to prepare for His return!

I believe intimacy and servanthood go hand in hand. There is a delicate balance that we need to manage wisely because the old phrase, "So busy doing the Lord's work we forgot about the Lord of the work" can easily slip into our operation.

Now note how Deborah sat under the "Palm of Deborah" in Judges 4:4. To me this sounds an idyllic, peaceful, restful place, perhaps reminiscent of holidays in the sun, taking shade under palm trees. However, the main meaning of palm trees or palm leaves in the Bible is victory and celebration. What did people wave as Jesus entered Jerusalem? Palm leaves.

The place of intimacy with God is a place which gives us the strength to obtain victory.

It's in that quiet place where we focus on what God says about us and our lives that our attitude and outlook changes. We begin to see ourselves as God sees us. We begin to stand firm on the promises He declares over our lives. We begin to gain wisdom and understanding for the journey ahead.

Palm trees are often found growing in deserts. Isn't that amazing – that something so beautiful and majestic could grow in a place of drought? Apparently it is because the palm tree doesn't waste its resources on growing branches but focuses on distributing the resources to the leaves that crown the top of the trunk. I wonder how much more we could achieve if we focused our resources?

The Palm of Deborah was situated between Ramah and Bethel. Ramah we know means "high place". Verses 4-5 go on to say that these two cities were within the hilly region of Ephraim. Ramah was also the place we read of in Jeremiah 31:15: *"A voice was heard in Ramah, lamentation and bitter weeping: Rachel weeping for her children, refused to be comforted for her children because they were not."* Bethel, of course, means "House of God" and again the story of Genesis 28 where Jacob realises Bethel is no longer a "certain place" but an "awesome place" is explored in my husband's book, *From Beach Hut to Palace*.

So somewhere between the hilly, high, difficult place of weeping and despair and the House of God lies the Palm of Deborah. Perhaps we all need to take shelter and take stock at the Palm of Deborah!

This is all very conceptual. I have told you I believe that serving is a gateway to intimacy with God and that intimacy with God is necessary if we are to be effective leaders, but how can it be achieved you may ask!

Speaking as a mother I believe we need to be creative in finding those "Palm of Deborah" moments. For those of you who have ever had small children at home you will understand that those moments are pretty much unlikely to just happen! We have to make them happen if we agree they are necessary. For me, what worked when I had two pre-school children at home was that I created "book time". My youngest was still in need of a day time sleep; my eldest wasn't. I explained to him that every afternoon while his little brother slept he would have "book time". He could choose some books – normally that was about 20 – sit on his bed and "read" them until Mummy came back in. This gave me some time to open my Bible. I have often had sniggers when suggesting this idea to people and comments such as, "My child would never do that." My answer is, "No, of course they won't, if that's what you've decided." The Bible encourages us to "train a child", so do this by making it a positive experience; build it up from 5 mins to 20 mins; reward them afterwards; let them know that it's not optional – this is what's happening.

Just because you are a mother does not mean you have an excuse, a get-out clause not to have times with God. I don't see that written anywhere in the Bible! But God has given you a brain in order to be creative. A mother once told me she couldn't possibly find two minutes in her day to read the Bible. I asked her if she read the Bible with her toddler before bed. She confessed that she didn't, but took the challenge to begin to do this. Before long she found it wasn't just her daughter who was benefitting from the Bible stories, but she was also hearing God through those words she read to her daughter.

If you are a leader and a mother the cracks will soon begin to show if you are not spending time in God's Word. Later in this section I will address the importance also of serving in the House of God as a mother, but let me conclude this section by encouraging you as a mother and a leader to find time under the Palm of Deborah. You may be a busy bee like Deborah – good, that's what God wants you to be – but to achieve that victory you need to seek out shelter under the palm. If you are stuck between Ramah and Bethel, take time out in the Palm of Deborah.

QUALITY 2: DEVOTION

I believe Deborah also understood devotion. Let me explain. Devotion, how is it outworked? What is devotion? Is it a type of worship? Yes. Is it a time set aside for God? Kind of! When I think of what I am devoted to in my life, really it's God, my family and my church. These are the things I live and would die for.

Let's take my family. How does devotion outwork itself? Well, my devotion to my kids means I do things for them. I try to be the best mother; I spend time with them; I take them to school; I think about what's for tea; when I go shopping I think about what food is good for them and what food they will enjoy; I mend the broken toy; I sit with them when they are ill. Basically, I serve them. I may sometimes whinge about this, especially after a night time tummy bug causes lack of sleep, a lot of mess and me to catch the bug! However, I do consider it a privilege and a joy and I certainly wouldn't want it any other way.

Perhaps you are devoted to a worthy cause? A few years ago I did the Race for Life. What an amazing sight to see thousands of women all running a race for one cause – to beat cancer.

Last night I watched the news as protesters camped out on a roundabout in their town, adamant that the council shouldn't change it to traffic lights – not a cause that I get excited about, but these campers were adamant they were not moving until they got assurance their roundabout was staying. They were devoted to the cause.

I hope that in picking up this book you too are devoted to the cause of Jesus Christ and you understand that this is worked out through His Church. If not, let me encourage you that it is the only cause worth being devoted to! All other causes may have varying degrees of value, but the cause of Jesus Christ stands firm forever and is the only cause that guarantees eternal salvation and peace with God. Based on this premise, let's explore what devotion to the cause of Jesus Christ looks like.

Swinging back to the story of Deborah, let's pick up at Judges 4:6-9 NIV:

"She sent for Barak son of Abinoam from Kedesh in Naphtali and said to him, 'The Lord, the God of Israel, commands you: "Go, take with you ten thousand men of Naphtali and Zebulun and lead the way to Mount Tabor. I will lure Sisera, the commander of Jabin's army, with his chariots and his troops to the Kishon River and give him into your hands."'

Barak said to her, 'If you go with me, I will go; but if you don't go with me, I won't go.'

'Very well,' Deborah said, 'I will go with you. But because of the way you are going about this, the honour will not be yours, for the Lord will hand Sisera over to a woman.' So Deborah went with Barak to Kedesh."

I believe these verses show that Deborah was devoted to the service of Israel. She believed in the cause. King Jabin had "cruelly oppressed the Israelite for twenty years" (Judges 4:3).

This was something to be passionate about. She had personally witnessed the oppression of her people for twenty years. She was prepared to do something about it.

Remember she had the heart of a mother? Several years ago one of my sons became the victim of some bullying at school. I felt he was treated unfairly by both his teachers and the head teacher who failed to rise up in the situation. I wasn't happy! I was passionate about the cause of my son as he came home day after day with a "bump note" in his pocket. I became more and more devoted to ensure this cause was sorted. It lasted about a month until my son, following his father's advice, decided to give the bully a taste of his own medicine in the form of his fist neatly landing on the bully's chin. My mother's heart wanted it sorted! It was unfair. I hated to see my son suffer. I believe this is what Deborah felt for the Israelites. Their cause had continued for 20 long years, but it was her mother's heart that arose when she heard the call from God and without hesitation was devoted to sorting the cause.

She understood the importance of this word from God. Let me explain. Canaan was the land that God had intended for Israel since their escape from Egypt.

Exodus 3:8 NIV: *"So I have come down to rescue them from the hand of the Egyptians and to bring them up out of that land into a good and spacious land, a land flowing with milk and honey – the home of the Canaanites, Hittites, Amorites, Perizzites, Hivites and Jebusites."*

Looking later in Numbers we see the threat that existed if these nations weren't driven out:

"But if you do not drive out the inhabitants of the land, those you allow to remain will become barbs in your eyes and thorns in your sides. They will give you trouble in the land where you will live. And then I will do to you what I plan to do to them." (Numbers 33:55-56)

So Deborah would have had the understanding that whilst Israel was away from God they would be succumbing to the practices of the Canaanites, fully aware they were forfeiting their God-given destiny, including worship of baals. But when Israel was living in obedience to God she understood that these nations needed to be driven out to enable them to live in the fullness of all God had in store for them.

She realised it was not a small task that God was asking of Barak and thus her attitude, when Barak asked her to go with him, was not surprising:

"Very well I will go with you." (Judges 4:9)

She had every excuse in the book a prophetess needed to "seek" God: she had a role, a title, people needed her to be under the Palm of Deborah, she was a woman for goodness' sake, not built for fighting, and she was a mother. However, none of these excuses came into play. She simply said, "Very well, I will go with you."

She was devoted to the purposes of God being outworked. If you are a leader you will, I am sure, have a deep set conviction in your heart, a devotion that compels you to respond to the big asks from God; to stand up and make a difference; to pay the price and to say to your kids, "Hold on tight, we're going on a journey!"

Once, a leader who was facing a stretching challenge said to me, "Becky, you don't understand. I cannot respond because I am called to my kids."

At the time I found this quite offensive. My private thoughts were, "Are you saying I am *not* called to my kids?" But the more I thought about this statement the more I understood that this is the basic calling of any mother, Christian or not – to be called to our kids. Surely that is the most fundamental lesson of motherhood?

Our Family Stream Pastor puts it so well: "What are you devoted to? Your children or your children in the House of God?"

I am delighted to say that the leader overcame her challenges and now stands strong in the House of God with an understanding that she is called to serve in the House alongside her children, modelling devotion to the cause of Christ for her children to rise up and follow.

If you are a leader you will have an understanding of calling; it burns in you and you can't get away from it. Some people may not understand it, they may not get it, you may be told you're doing it all wrong, you may be told your kids are suffering, you may be told you're going over the top – do you really need to be at church all the time? Does church really need to dominate your whole life? When this happens you need to be all the more certain of your calling and devotion.

If you are wavering and questioning your devotion to the House of God let me pose the following to you:

These days most mothers are working mothers as well as raising a family. That may be in church employment or elsewhere. The question I want to pose is this: how do you feel about leaving your children to go to work? I assume you would reason that, if it were possible, you'd prefer to be at home with your children or, if they are school age, to be able to take and collect them from school each day. Yet you know it's necessary for you to work to put food on your table, to have holidays and to clothe your family. So you rationalise it in your head: I am doing this for the greater good of my child and our family. Yes?

Now ask yourself if you are willing to leave your children with babysitters to attend a team meeting, a training night at church, an event serving others in your city. Ouch! Have you ever thought that leaving your children to serve the purposes of God has eternal consequences for you and your children, whereas going to work has only short term benefits? Read that again:

Ask yourself if you are willing to leave your children with babysitters to attend a team meeting, a training night at church or an event serving others in your city ... leaving your children to serve the purposes of God has eternal consequences for you and your children. Going to work has only short term benefits.

Do you want your kids to grow up in a great church? Have a look at your priorities. Don't feel guilty just because it's not a paid job, we are talking about serving the King of Kings; we are talking about modelling serving God to your children. Someone has to pay the price!

I don't know what kind of church you are in but I believe BCCers are so blessed. There are great kids' facilities and a whole host of great kids' ministries all ready to bless families and their children. This is wonderful and I wouldn't want it any other way. The downside is that we can become consumerist, lazy, mothers!

My previous church was a small church plant. If I wanted something for my kids I had to do it! Someone always has to pay the price. How about you step up and help carry the weight, set an example for other mothers and your children and help provide great facilities for those parents and children who are living without hope?

Our arrival in Stoke on Trent was interesting as my children were 18 months and four at the time. Please understand that moving to Stoke on Trent was as foreign to me as moving to the other side of the world. I am a Southerner. I had never heard of Stoke on Trent until I met my husband and had rarely travelled that far "north". I am now beginning to understand Stoke is not north, but in the Midlands! We had left all we knew, everyone we knew, our team, our family, our security and our reputation in South Wales.

On arrival at what was "The Bethel" it was pretty evident that it was going to be a full on job to get this thing working how we believed church should be. Therefore me having a comfortable, "stay at home" mum's existence was not an option – not that I ever would have wanted that, although sometimes I'm curious as to what it must be like! It was going to take all our time and energy. So my mantra, explained in the introduction, became "We are called as a family." The boys literally came to every meeting. I had no other option; I didn't know anyone who I could ask to babysit. At one evening meeting the boys were there, once again, in their pyjamas.

After the meeting I was in the coffee area with them and a lady (a very well-meaning lady, I'm sure) came up to me and said, "Those poor children, they should be at home in bed."

I held my tongue but everything in me wanted to say, "Shall I tell you a little about my life and the challenges we are currently facing?"

If I had not had the conviction of heart that I was doing the right thing for my God, if I had not been devoted to the cause, this comment could have thrown me off guard. However, my attitude, as I'm sure yours would be, was, *"As for me and my house, we'll serve the Lord"* (Joshua 24:15). As a mother I have to outwork that how I see best.

That period of our lives didn't last forever, it was only a season. I thank God that now we have a wonderful team of babysitters who love my kids and consider it an honour to look after them when we are not able to. But my prayer is that during that period of our lives our kids learnt to love the House of God, not despise it; that they considered it an honour and a privilege to be in the House of God while other children were asleep at home.

As a church we use Twitter heavily to communicate effectively. Our Communications Director will, from time to time, release new hash tags to help explain who we are as a church. There is one I love: #IamBCC. To me it helps explain my life. I am a mum, I am a wife, I am a daughter, I am an employee, I am a follower of God, I am my church. No order, just I AM.

Please let me share this story with you which I believe shows how the quality of devotion can be outworked.

Raising Kids versus Raising Kids in the House of God

BY MANDY SIDLEY – MINISTRIES EXEC
& FAMILY STREAM PASTOR

I consider myself blessed beyond measure! Our family is serving and doing life in a church that God is building for the next generation. As families it is so important that we see the needs we have and look for a church that can help us grow, both together and individually. At Breathe City Church I see many examples of God working with families and causing them to flourish. This transformation does not happen without willingness and an openness to the biblical principles God has set out for us.

Our journey has not always been the most comfortable, but it has been the most rewarding. Only a short while ago my husband had the honour of baptising our children on confession of their own faith in God. As I said, blessed beyond measure!

I am the Ministries Executive at Breathe City Church and my husband, Michael, is the director of a logistics company. I work part time, Michael works full time and together we serve on the Primary Leadership team. We have two children, Samuel, aged 8, and Bronte, aged 6. As you can imagine, our lives are full on.

When we began our journey serving in the House of God, I can remember thinking that we would allow so much time for this and so much time for that ... we would give two nights a week to the things we felt passionate about. Have you ever tried to live your life in compartments? Let me tell you, it only leads to frustration. The truth of it is that God wants your attention all the time! When you make the decision to follow God it's not exclusively for Sunday mornings. Neither is it to fit in with your agendas. Not at all!

It's you. God wants you!

God is working towards your wholeness, individually, as a couple, as parents and as a family.

When we had this revelation that our lives weren't meant to line up with those around us, it was brilliant, exciting even! We were not called to a great adventure within our own rules, where's the adventure in that?! No, it's letting go and letting God have charge over every area of life.

I love that our children are in relationship with such a lot of people and being part of a large church. They see people engaging in worship, they see people serving, they see people who were in the children's programmes that they are in go into all areas of serving in the House. They see the momentum and growth in others. They serve on Lovestoke, our social outreach programme. They themselves are being the change in the communities in which they live. They see the fruit of BCC's partnership ministry, Compassion, in Uganda and they pray for the children that we sponsor and will hopefully visit them, just as their cousins (also part of BCC!) already have. And the list goes on...

What I love most is that, for our children, this is not a learnt behaviour, but a lifestyle. They will grow up knowing how to be a Christian, not only spiritually but in action too. They will automatically understand that their faith has to be outworked, that God expects us all to see the fruit of our labours.

So in answer to the question of raising kids versus raising kids in the House of God, I would say, where else would I rather them be? We could be the most fantastic parents in the world, but because of the limitations of experience, wisdom, knowledge and background, we could not possibly give our children the varied and whole view of life they need to be all God wants them to be. In a healthy and safe environment we are seeing children thrive in the House of God. They are being loved for who they are and inspired to become all they can be.

QUALITY 3: RESPONSE

I have already explained that Deborah responded to God and to her fellow believers' request and she refused to be confined by excuses. Let's explore this issue further, which I believe cripples so many women.

At BCC we have worked very hard to eliminate a culture of excuse across the board. We have had to battle through the ingrained "Stokie" negative mindset. One of our cultural pillars as a house is to be "Positive". We work hard at training our people to be positive. This may not be an issue for you, but in a city which prides itself in its depravity, unemployment and violence it was, as a church, very necessary to be counter-cultural. Of course, the message of the Gospel is one of faith, hope and love, one of speaking life and positivity into a hurt and dying world. I am sure negativity is not just an issue for Stokies; I am sure it is a mindset that many battle with and mothers in particular can succumb so easily to this damaging mindset.

Phrases like, "It's a nightmare ... It's the end of the world ... I just can't cope ... I'm losing the plot..." are used all too flippantly. Then, of course, you have the "toddler group syndrome" which breeds a downwards spiral of negativity in mothers. Anyone who's ever attended a pre-school toddler group must know what I am talking about. When I first ventured to our local toddler group with my first child I went reluctantly, but with the intention that it would be good for my child.

What I didn't realise was how bad it would be for me!

The experience, as I'm sure many will agree, is as horrific as a school disco. Chairs around the edge, toys in the middle and the mix of shy, pushy, opinionated and relaxed parents created an atmosphere of utter chaos among the children. It ranged from sharing being demanded to snatching being ignored, screaming and crying, running about and running over one another – absolute pandemonium!

Then it was "song time". For my eldest this was a treat because he knew it meant a drink of squash and biscuit (I never let him have squash at home). However, for my slightly more vocal second child, "song time" was an experience which ensured we never returned to that toddler group again! The cup was too difficult to suck from so he threw it on the floor with a big scream in the middle of Grandma Betty's rendition of "Wind the Bobbin Up".

The child next to him took the last biscuit and that was the final straw – he had a complete melt down and everyone knew about it! I scooped him up and legged it out of there as fast as I could, never to return again!

The worst part of this experience was not the fact my child misbehaved, that's what children do and it's our job to teach them how to behave. It was the looks from other mothers, some pitying, some glaring as if to say, "Shut your child up!" Surely we're all in this together? Surely we should be supporting and encouraging one another? Surely no one's child is perfect all the time?!

The other negativity that drove me away from toddler groups was the "comparison conversations". Any parent knows where I am going with this: "What, your son hasn't cut his first tooth? That's ever so late..." making you begin to wonder if you better make a trip to the dentist in case your child may be toothless for life.

"Have you got your child's name down for the best high school? No? You're joking! You know they'll never achieve any GCSEs if they go to the other one..." making you believe that your child is doomed to be an academic failure.

Then there's the walking issue, the breastfeeding issue, the organic food issue, the list goes on ... But if, like me, you come away from these environments feeling thoroughly negative, please do something about it and make sure you replace the negativity with a positive mindset for your child. I often make my boys repeat after me, "I'm a winner, I'm a champion and I'm a leader." I am sure it does me as much good as it does them!

I am so glad BCC doesn't do toddler groups but does have a thriving Cafe Kids ministry where, each month, thousands of parents and children are loved for who they are and inspired to become all the can be. I thank God that many other church leaders have come to look at this ministry and modelled something similar in their churches.

Surrounding yourself in a negative culture will have one outcome – you will become negative. That negativity will rub off into all areas of your life. It's my opinion that the two most excuse-driven sectors of our society are mothers and students.

I once chatted with a church leader who was struggling to break through. She complained about the pressures put on her by the congregation and then exclaimed, "Don't they understand I've got children?" I understand where she was coming from. Leaders' wives, who may also be leaders in their own right, can often be put under a huge amount of pressure, possibly unintentionally by a congregation. They can be expected to be all things to their kids, husband and church. However, the statement "But I've got children" to me is an excuse! It's as lame as saying, "But I've got a dog" or "But I've got chicken pox."

Deal with the issue rather than use your children as an excuse.

I would be devastated if my children grew up thinking they were my excuse. I would be devastated if my children grew up without me modelling what it is to serve in the House of God.

Sometimes the excuse may be a cover for some women. Children are a great security blanket to hide behind! If you're feeling a little nervous or challenged a child is a great "get out clause"! Can I challenge you: your children won't be children forever and then what? Don't hide behind your children, God has called you!

Now let's address some other common excuses that parents give to serving in the House of God. I do apologise if I am being rather challenging, but you picked up this book!

"My child misses out on things..."

"The children have football, ballet, parties..."

"My child can't sit still in church; I'll come when she's older..."

The simple answer to these excuses is: make a choice as to what you are serving, or should I say *who* you are serving!

Again, *"As for me and my house we will serve the Lord"* (Joshua 24:15).

My children know that if a party invite comes home for a Sunday morning it's not even up for discussion. I am under no illusion – my children will not miss out by not going to that party. I firmly believe, *"Better is one day in your courts than a thousand elsewhere"* (Psalm 84:10) and this is what I want my children to grow up understanding.

My youngest child recently questioned a new believer whose child was engaging in a non-church activity on a Sunday. Aged six he said, "Don't his parents understand that church comes first?" I, of course, explained his parents had recently only come to know Jesus and it is a journey of understanding that church comes first. I believe that, with this attitude sowed in at an early age, he will grow to be a strong and mighty warrior in the House of God.

We recently had some decisions to make. Through a variety of circumstances, several evenings became free from after school activities for my eldest son. He asked if he could join the local Cubs group that his school friends went to. I was aware that this particular Cubs group was of a similar vein to the toddler group I described earlier. Comparison conversations and pushy parents seemed prevalent. I have a long history with and admiration for the Scouting and Guiding movements, growing up as a Girl Guide and achieving the Queen's Guide, the highest award in girl guiding for you ignorant people! My Grandfather also received an MBE from the Queen for his service to Scouting. I like the movement, I like its values and I think it's a great activity for children. However, it's not a cause that I am devoted to. It's not a cause that I would want to precede church in my son's life. After investigation we found out that my son would soon be old enough for Scouts which met on a Friday night – the same night as our church's kids' and youth programmes.

To me it's a no brainer!

What influences do I want in my child's life: that of a very good organisation or that of the Lord of Lords and King of Kings?

If I compromise on this, then what does it show my son?

What's next on the slippery slope?

Not attending church?

Being influenced by his school friends rather than those who love Jesus?

God is so good and rewards the faithful. I heard of another Scout group meeting locally on a Monday evening, a laid back village group that appears to have a lack of pushy parents and comparison conversations. Of course, my son was disappointed not to go to the same group as his school friends, but he's loving his Monday night Cubs and I hope the journey, which I involved him in every step of the way, is part of his personal decision to ensure the House of God always comes first in his life.

There is nothing sadder than when you see a mother invest in her children while excluding God's House then wonder why they grow up away from God. I am talking about the parents who decide that their "talented child" must attend football training on a Sunday morning or dancing classes instead of kids' church activities. Is it any wonder their children grow up away from God? You may feel I'm ignorant making such statements as my children are not yet teenagers and there will come a time when they will have to make their own decisions. I understand that.

When that happens, all I can do is stand back, watch and pray. But when that time comes I want to be satisfied that I have done all I can to help them understand the importance of God's House.

Thinking back to the leader who excused herself for having children, let me pose another thought. Your children are your children, why should church be negatively impacted? Sometimes it's appropriate for roles to change in the different stages of your life, but what should remain constant is your commitment to serving in the House of God, particularly if you are a leader.

Too many mothers drop the ball when they get pregnant. I will never forget a wise lady who decided to embarrass me at a youth conference I was leading. As she questioned me as to why I wasn't getting involved in the afternoon's water fight, I replied, "I am pregnant, you know."

She responded, "Becky, pregnancy is not an ailment, it's a gift from God." Of course, she said it in jest. I am sure getting involved in a full blown water fight with 200 teenagers is not the best activity to engage in when you are pregnant. But her words are so true. Pregnancy is not an ailment – it is a gift from God. Why do we think it's okay to drop off church activity when we are pregnant? Why should others have to carry the load because of a decision we've made?

Whilst writing this book I am half way through my pregnancy with number three. It is rather comical that God should decide I need a more practical outworking of this subject as I am writing about it! I am now feeling those welcome "kicks". I was reminded recently how I believe a baby's ear becomes attuned to the Word of God whilst they are still in the womb. When I had my first child we were amazed when our then pastor, who also happened to be my father-in-law, came to visit the baby. As he reached out to hold the baby, he spoke and my son physically turned his face to him. I am convinced he knew his voice. Of course, you would expect a newborn baby to recognise Mum's voice, maybe Dad's, and sometimes brothers or sisters. But week after week my unborn child had heard the "man of God's" voice through a microphone as I sat in church listening to him preach. This makes me stand in awe as a mum, aware of the responsibility we have to our children before they are even born to keep church central.

Who do you want your child to turn their face towards, the man of God or the TV show host? Secular music? The football coach? I pray my sons will always turn their faces to the words of men and women of God.

I had a similar experience with music. When my child struggled sleeping, different people suggested that I try music. Being a good youth leader at the time the music I had to hand was lively worship music. I never looked back. It would always soothe my child. Once I was visiting my parents and they didn't have a CD player in the bedroom where my son was sleeping. My mum suggested using the radio and putting Classic FM on instead. At the young age of just a few months old my son knew the difference. His ears were not tuned to Classic FM but to the sound of God's saints praising – again, quite probably because he'd heard it week after week whilst in the womb. Never underestimate how your actions affect your child!

I hope I have banished any excuses you may have been hoarding when it comes to serving God with children, but allow me finish on this sombre note. In many church circles women have lost the right to minister in church. Is it any wonder when we've spent years moaning, "I've got children to look after!" No! They are a blessing from God, not an ailment to complain about!

I think it's fair to say that Deborah beat the excuse culture! We have already mentioned that she had every excuse under the sun not to go to battle with Barak, but no air time is given to these excuses. Imagine an army of mighty women who refuse to succumb to the excuse culture!

I'm in!

Will you join me?

The next Senior Pastor may be in City Kids: Church

QUALITY 4: HEART FOR THE NEXT GENERATION

At BCC, part of our vision statement says that we a building a church that is generational. As a church we believe that this is important because too many great works of God come to a halt when the "man of God" leading them retires or moves on. We base our operation on the fact that the next Senior Pastor may be in our City Kids: Church right now!

This changes the value that we put on our kids and youth facilities!

Deborah may or may not have been a natural mother, but she certainly had a heart for the younger generation. In her song in Judges 5, she begins by talking about princes and praises God for them taking the lead. It appears to excite her that the young men are rising up as leaders:

"When the princes in Israel take the lead, when the people willingly offer themselves – praise the Lord!" (Judges 5:2)

She goes onto express in verse 9, *"My heart is with Israel's princes with the willing volunteers among the people."*

I love it when I see the children and young people of BCC serving and taking steps towards becoming leaders. I remember one occasion when two of our young lads walked past City Kids: Church and noticed a City Kids Pastor setting up the venue alone. Aged only nine or ten they apparently went and asked the City Kids Pastor if she needed any help.

I love this! Just as it appears Deborah loved to see the young "princes" rising up.

Everyone at BCC is encouraged to serve on a team. The last session of our Connect (new to church) course is given over to our Volunteer Pastor who presents the opportunities for serving and signs people up on the spot! However, what I find truly wonderful is the number of children and young people we have serving on teams. It is common place to find children as young as four wearing a red Embrace Team (welcome team) t-shirt. My own son started serving in the Communications Stream as soon as he could read well. Now, aged nine, he can competently operate Song Pro and has a good understanding of the importance of communications within church. This opportunity for children and young people to serve is facilitated by a team of adult staff and volunteers who have a heart for the next generation.

What a crying shame when kids have a desire to serve in the House of God and that desire is quashed with comments such as, "You're too young" or "You're not good enough yet." I believe Deborah had the understanding of a mother that the young people were the future of Israel and everything she did was to help them in the future.

It's no wonder we see in verse 15, *"The Princes of Issachar were with Deborah."* "Princes" or children will always want to follow those who have a heart for them. Having a heart for the next generation is so important because this attracts children to the House of God. Imagine the child who turns up at church, is told to be quiet, to sit still, is scowled at, talked over, doesn't understand the preaching and is quickly ushered out at the end of the service. Sadly, this is the experience of many children visiting church. Is it any wonder that we have a problem of aging congregations in our nation?

I recently took my neighbours' kids to church with us. As we got in the car I said to my boys, "Do you want to tell your friends what church will be like?" One of my neighbours' kids said, "Don't worry, we know it'll be as boring as school assembly." My kids tried to correct him, but I don't think it was until he sat down, saw the video presentations, the lights, heard the loud music and witnessed everyone around him bouncing that he realised "church" was not like school assembly. It wasn't long before he was joining in with a smile on his face. It's so important that children have a good experience of church; that they enjoy it; that we allow them to take ownership.

My kids love to be involved in this journey with us. My eldest spent his first four years of life on the set up team for our church which never had its own building. When we moved to Stoke, aged four, the first time he walked into the auditorium he looked at the ceiling and noticed the projector attached. He said, "Mummy, that's not going to be very easy to set down." At that young age he knew how church worked (well "set up church" as he called it). Often, he will be the first to notice a change in the start-up DVD, the musical arrangement or a change in the run sheet.

One evening, during the early days of repurposing the church, a phone call came through in the evening to inform us that someone had left the church. The children were upstairs in bed, asleep so I thought! I took the call then recounted to James that "so and so" had decided to leave the church. The next thing I knew my eldest son was sat on the sofa saying, "So Mummy, what are we going to do about this?"

I love this for two reasons. Firstly, he was taking ownership – he felt the problem was as much his as ours (of course, we let him know he didn't need to worry about it). Secondly, this is leadership training. In seeing how James and I handled that situation it is (hopefully!) preparing him and teaching him how to handle similar situations in the future, should he choose and be called to be a leader in the House of God.

Many leaders try to hide the "nasty" bits of church life from their kids and I agree there is unfortunately some stuff that goes on in church that I would not want to expose my kids to. However, we never purposefully hide the day to day function of church from our kids.

If we are called as a family then we are in this together.

I am happy for them to see the lows as long as they see the highs as well. It is through these times that their faith and understanding in God will increase. I believe my sons are called to be leaders in some capacity. Where that happens is between them and God, but hopefully by watching us as leaders they can learn from our mistakes as well as from our successes. Then maybe, when their turn comes, they can start from a more advantaged position than we did.

I have found it challenging involving my kids in some of our ministries. Women may be suffering life-controlling issues, escaping abuse, escaping addictions and many other issues that cause them not to be the woman of strength that God desires them to be. Particularly in the early days of setting up ministries my children would often be with me. They would witness women detoxing, they would chat to women who had just been released from prison, play with children who had just escaped an abusive father. Normally these are not the type of life experiences that you want your children to experience. But two years on from the opening of this facility my children now meet the same women and see their lives transformed.

We've so got to involve our kids in this journey called Church! They are called to be salt and light just like we are! If you protect them and leave them ill-informed then someone else will educate them. I would way prefer my kids see a recovering heroin addict through the eyes of God's healing power rather than witness it at a drunken teenage party.

Parents: you are your children's primary role model when it comes to church. What do you want your kids to think of church? Then start talking it. I want kids to feel like church is "home". I want church to be the first place they turn to in times of trouble, unhappiness, difficulty or confusion as they grow older.

One of my most difficult childhood times was when my friend was killed in a road accident. I was 18 at the time and on the eve of his accident, not sure if he would live or die, the one place I wanted to be was in the House of God. It felt safe.

Is it any wonder that the child gets to be a teenager and decides to stop going to church when all they have heard for the last 13 years is Mum and Dad pulling church apart over the dinner table?

But what do you say to the mother who did all the right things, had a heart for the next generation and gave her kids a positive experience of church, but her teenage kids are back sliding? I believe that mother needs to be encouraged that she did the right thing and that every child, when they grow up, has to decide for themselves and keep believing and praying that the good seeds sown will reap a harvest. Never ever should that mother beat herself up about being too committed to God!

I wonder how Deborah felt when the "princes" at the start of Chapter 6 "did evil in the eyes of the Lord". Devastated I would imagine. She is not mentioned again in the book of Judges. Maybe she had died by this point. Would we question whether her heart for the princes was a waste of time and energy? Certainly not! Maybe it was one of those princes who became the next Judge, who knows? Maybe the seeds that you sow today may just raise up in the next generation a mighty man or woman of God? Maybe two, maybe ten or even hundreds!

Proverbs 22:6: *"Train up a child in the way he should go..."* What way should your child go? I believe my children are called for great things in God, so age appropriately I will use our leadership life to train them. I believe, like Deborah, God has a huge heart for the next generation. Let's get on board!

Before we go on to look at our final quality, let me share another story of someone I believe outworks these last two qualities that we have discussed.

We are Called as a Family
BY SARA PASS – CITY PASTOR

I have always loved to be in God's House. I remember as a young child crying when my dad went to leadership meetings because I wanted to go too. One night I even secretly followed my mum to a Bible Study. She only realised when she got there that I was right behind! Needless to say, I quickly got taken home! Even at this young age I had the desire to be there – in the House of my God.

This sense of wanting to be in and serve in God's House grew as I went through my teenage years into being a young woman. I knew that this was what I wanted for my family too, but when

I was pregnant with my first child, I found that not everybody thought the same as me! People made comments to me such as, "You need to let go now Sara" or "You need to slow down ... You need to put yourself first." I lived with a sense of guilt, wanting to be a great mum, but not wanting to let go of serving in God's House.

My revelation came when Pastor Becky recently spoke to the mums at BCC. She spoke of being called as a family. It wasn't a choice of being a great mum OR serving God. It was doing the two things together.

I felt liberated!

It was around the same time that Mark and I were asked to lead a regional congregation as part of BCC. We chose to do this as a family: myself, Mark and our children Summer, aged 9 and Toby, 7. So our children were involved from the start. They came to the very first prayer meeting that we held for this new venture. They read the Bible during the devotion and they were encouraged by all present to be involved. As a family we began to pray daily for BCC North. We encouraged the children to pray specifically for what we were doing. They soon began to ask questions like, "What are we believing for this week Mum?" "What are we going to do next?"

We were modelling a passion for God's House and our children were following. They copied our model! So we carried on. The children now hear us encouraging our team, they take part in the prayer walks for our area of the city, they come to the meetings.

Summer has grown so much in her faith through this that now, when adults share prophetic words, she will share what she feels God has said to her. It is wonderful to watch and to listen.

We want to help all the families at BCC to feel like they are in this together. We want the children to have ownership of the things we are doing. As adults we share ideas with them and ask for their opinions. This belongs to them too, this is their home. I'll always remember the week where we broke 100 people in attendance at BCC North. I was on the front row with Summer and Toby and the call came forward ... 95 people ... we sang the first song ... 99 ... and again ... 103 then, 105! Summer and Toby were just as excited as we were; they were in this as much as us!

Serving in God's House has always been of the utmost importance to me, it's what we are commanded to do in the Bible and it's what Mark and I wanted to do ourselves and with our children. Often in churches serving seems to be for adults, but at BCC there is a culture where children are encouraged to serve too. So our children serve. Summer is part of the Embrace Team and Toby is part of Comms. This is where Toby has flourished. On a Sunday morning he is up at 6.00am and at church for 7.00am to help Mark and the team set up. He chooses to do this; he wants to do this; he can't wait to get to God's House!

I love that my kids are relaxed and confident in everything we are involved with at BCC. They are encouraged and empowered to be so. When we walk as a family into BCC, they are home! What joy, as a mum and dad, to see God at work in their lives. They are planted in His House and there they will flourish (Genesis 22:17).

QUALITY 5: STRENGTH

We have already addressed the issue of strength as we have looked at other biblical characters earlier in the book. However, Deborah's strength is that of a leader. This is a different calibre of strength in my opinion. The type of strength needed as a leader is an inner strength that needs to be very personal. As a leader you will experience things that you may not be able to share with others. If you are fortunate you will have one or two confidantes that you can share your inner most struggles with. But, unfortunately, the reality is that there may be some stuff you just can't share with anyone except God.

It doesn't appear that Deborah had any close allies that could encourage her to remain strong. There was Barak, but it seemed that she needed to be the strong one for him. It was her strength that carried him into battle. She even instructed him in the operations: *"Then Deborah said to Barak, 'Go! This is the day the Lord has given Sisera into your hands.'"* (Judges 4:14)

In this situation we see that Deborah takes authority. As a leader, strength comes in taking authority. The buck stops with you. I am sure Deborah would have been happy for Barak to take the lead and go into battle without her. I am sure this was one job she'd have been happy to delegate! But Barak wouldn't go alone and she'd heard from God – the job had to get done! So there was no option, she had to take authority.

Another clue to Deborah's strength as a leader is in Judges 5:19-21 NKJV: *"The kings came and fought, then the kings of Canaan fought in Taanach, by the waters of Megiddo; they took no spoils of silver. They fought from the heavens; the stars from their courses fought against Sisera. The torrent of Kishon swept them away, that ancient torrent, the torrent of Kishon. O my soul, march on in strength!"*

Kings are crawling out of the woodwork to fight, rivers are sweeping people away, it's pouring with rain and Deborah's response is "march on in strength!"

Oh, how we could learn from this attitude! I remember a particular summer when we'd had one difficulty after another at Breathe City Church. It was crunch time. Either God was going to come through or we were going under! Night after night James and I sat in bed not sleeping, drinking cups of tea encouraging ourselves to "march on my soul be strong" (NIV). But in reality we weren't feeling very strong! It felt more like the rivers and rain and those fighting against us were going to win this battle. But they didn't! And we did get through! We were strong enough and so are you!

I love Proverbs 14:4:

"From the strength of an ox comes an abundant harvest."

An ox is an animal that is trained to pull the plough. He's castrated so that he can focus on that purpose. The farmer wants an abundant harvest, of course he does, and his business relies on it. The ox is built for one purpose only: to bring in an abundant harvest.

I believe that God wants us to have an abundant harvest. During our early years in youth ministry people would say to us, "Just sow seeds in young people's lives. Others may reap them later, just be faithful in sowing the seeds."

I find this so discouraging! What farmer sows his seeds with the thought that someone else will reap the harvest?! The idea is ridiculous and he would soon be out of business!

I believe I am called to sow *and* reap. Thank God we did sow many seeds during our time in youth ministry, but I thank God even more for the harvest that was reaped through broken lives turning to Jesus and being restored! Several of those young people still stand alongside us in ministry and that gives me so much joy. It's how it should be!

But the Bible is clear that we will only reap a harvest if we have strength. Of course, it makes sense, strength to see things through, strength to stand by someone while they work out the mess in their life, strength to pay the cost of time, energy and finance.

How do we train ourselves to become as strong as an ox?

- Read the Bible, it's full of wisdom that shows us how to develop our strength.
- Take advice from godly advisors rather than those who are not aiming at the same destination as us.
- Be positive, look at things with a "can do" mindset! I am sure we would never have achieved anything as a church if we had not applied this principle! There will never be enough resources, finance, volunteers or time!

Remembering where our strength comes from is key:

"Your strength will come from settling down in complete dependence on me" (Isaiah 30:15)

We can depend on so many things, but it's only God who is fully dependable.

"I can do all things through Christ who strengthens me." (Philippians 4:13)

Let me finish with this quote from one of my favourite books, *Lioness Arising* by Lisa Bevere:

"Your journey through life is accompanied by many voices and influences. Some voices spur you onto places yet unknown and others hold you back.

There are voices from your past – family, disappointments and fear that intermittently yell and whisper, 'Turn aside, turn back. You might fail. You might get hurt.'

Amid these negative, life-draining voices is the call of the powerful life-giving voices. They are always present, but if you choose not to listen for them, you might miss them. The voices of the heavenly hosts who went before you call out through the scriptures cheering you forward and onward, 'Don't listen to the lies of your enemy who is condemned and tormented. Don't be distracted.

We need you!

Stay on course and run your race!'"

Epilogue

Alongside the other women of Breathe City Church, I am so blessed to be in a church where women, and the contribution that they bring to church life, are valued. I recently preached a challenging message to our men on Fathers' Day and was humbled at their response, which I think displays their attitude towards female leaders. However, I am well aware that this is not the experience for every woman in church life.

Please be encouraged: if you feel the call to leadership, you are not alone! It is real! And it's irrelevant if it's recognised or not. If leadership is who we are and not a title then be secure in that! Be a leader where you can, keep your heart right and believe that God will open a door for you at the correct time.

I once had a female leader come to be in tears saying, "But you don't understand Becky, I need to be on stage to lead, I need to preach, I need the congregation to see I'm a leader." I don't think this attitude helped her cause. Another great friend of mine was told, when she and her husband took over a church, that she would certainly not be allowed in the pulpit. Believing they were called to this denomination they agreed with the "rules" and have honoured them. You could not deny that this amazing lady is a leader and I am sure would be a great preacher. But, in the absence of having the pulpit, her leadership is outworked throughout wider church life where she serves alongside her husband, whether that be in Alpha courses, pastoring or coming alongside other leaders' wives in her denomination.

What a contrast in attitudes! Leadership is so much more than having the microphone!

Allow me to end with a devotion to the millions of women on Planet Earth who are on the journey that we have explored in this book.

I have met some of those women in my circle of influence and I am humbled by their resilience and determination to complete the race. When I look upon the journey of some women I stand in awe of the challenges that they are in the process of overcoming; challenges that I could only understand a little of, but nevertheless I stand with them in faith, hope and love knowing that *"Christ who began this work will bring it to completion"* (Philippians 1:6).

Let us be encouraged that life is full of seasons and each season brings blessings and challenges that we can choose to embrace or not. In embracing the challenges of each season I believe we are on the course to becoming the strong women that God designed us to be – the women whom without creation was not complete!

That's me and that's you!

What a calling!

Appendix

Stronger Mentors – Naomi

Stronger mentors are integral to a girl's success at Stronger. They provide one-to-one support that is not always possible from other staff or volunteers. They should be concerned with the practical and spiritual journey of the girl they are mentoring.

Remember, mentoring works best where a relationship is developed. Always think "Ruth and Naomi".

Where a girl has a child it may sometimes be appropriate to include the child in more informal sessions or to do something special for them.

Below are some steps to begin the spiritual journey with the girl you are mentoring:

1. Is she born again?

You can ask questions like, "Tell me about your Christian journey. Do you know God? When was the last time you spoke to God?"

2. Is she reading her Bible?

Ask questions like, "Do you have a Bible? When did you last read it? Do you find it easy to read?" You need to establish what Bible reading programme is appropriate. Encourage them to use the devotion time in the daily routine to be reading their Bible and praying. Ask them regularly how they are doing. You could ask them to text you a verse each week that speaks to them etc.

3. Prayer

Do they pray? What about? Encourage them to keep a journal of prayers and answers.

4. Developing their relationship with God

You should begin to notice this! As a mentor, the Stronger Reading List is available for you to choose books that you think are helpful for the girl you are mentoring. Please ensure you talk about the books and what they have learnt.

You can also spend time talking about preaches from Sunday and at other Breathe City Church events they have attended. Again, encourage them to take notes.

What is a Mentor? – Ruth

The Bible talks about a lady called Ruth. Ruth was so committed to seeking God that she gave up all she ever knew to go on a journey. She trusted fully in a God she hardly knew and though the beginning part of her journey was tough, God ended up giving her more than she could ever have dreamt of.

Ruth had a "mother" with whom she "journeyed on together" (Ruth 1:19). This mother believed in her, encouraged her, did life with her and prayed for her. Her name was Naomi. However, it was a two-way relationship and Ruth also responded to Naomi's advice, looked upon her like a mother, encouraged her and prayed for her too. Whilst at Stronger you will have a Naomi, in the form of your mentor. She has committed to be your Naomi for two years.

Appendix

Your mentor will:
- Meet with you weekly
- Talk through "Disciple" (BCC's own Bible Study/Devotion)
- Chat with you about any concerns
- Share with you in achievements
- Guide you in choosing Christian resources to read.

Your Mentor will ask that you:
- Are open and honest
- Meet when agreed
- Share your concerns
- Share your achievements
- Respond to advice that she offers you.